147 Practical Tips

for
Synchronous
and Blended
Technology
Teaching and Learning

Rosemary M. Lehman and Richard A. Berg

Atwood Publishing
Madison, WI

Companion Web Site Home Page:
http://www.uwex.edu/disted/trans/htmltrials/147tips/index.html

[Note: Resources and URLs are integrated throughout the online text.]

Site Map and Access Keys
http://www.uwex.edu/disted/training/pubs/147tips/map.htm
Accessibility Statement
http://www.uwex.edu/disted/training/pubs/147tips/statement.htm

147 Practical Tips for Synchronous and Blended Technology Teaching and Learning
By Rosemary M. Lehman and Richard A. Berg

© 2007, Atwood Publishing, Madison, WI
www.atwoodpublishing.com

Cover design by Tamara Dever, TLC Graphics
www.tlcgraphics.com

Library of Congress Cataloging-in-Publication Data

Lehman, Rosemary M., 1932-
    147 practical tips for synchronous and blended technology teaching and learning /
Rosemary M. Lehman and Richard A. Berg.
        p. cm.
    ISBN 978-1-891859-69-4 (pb)
    1. Distance education. 2. Distance education—Computer-assisted instruction. 3. Teacher
effectiveness. 4. Educational planning. I. Berg, Richard A., 1968- II. Title. III. Title: One
hundred forty-seven practical tips for synchronous and blended technology teaching and
learning.

    LC5800.L47 2007
    371.35—dc22
                        2007026296

TABLE OF CONTENTS

ACKNOWLEDGMENTS

The tips in this book can help you learn and easily recall what is important to know and use when you teach or learn with synchronous and blended technologies. These tips are embedded in a framework of Pre-planning, Planning, Developing, Implementing, and Evaluating. They have been created and honed through years of research, professional development, and work in educational, governmental, non-profit, and business settings. All those we have learned from and worked with over the years we consider "tip partners." They have been an integral part of the process. Although it's impossible to acknowledge them here—there are tens of thousands—we want to note the significant role they have played in our work and offer our appreciation and thanks! And, thank you to Linda Babler of Atwood Publishing for the opportunity to add to the valuable *147 Tips Series* and editor William Cody for his keen eye and editorial expertise. We have enjoyed working with you.

The "we" we're speaking of is Instructional Communications Systems (ICS). ICS is a full service instructional design and support unit of University of Wisconsin-Extension. From audioconferencing to videoconferencing, webconferencing to webcasting, and instant messaging to mobile devices, ICS has the technology and the experience to meet the needs of distance learning and telecommunications for governmental, educational, and non-profit colleagues. Located in The Pyle Center, UW-Extension's conference and distance education center in Madison, Wisconsin, ICS is perfectly situated to accommodate distance learning and telecommunications needs. The Pyle Center's exceptional meeting space and leading-edge technology offer flexibility to provide the perfect learning environment—wherever clients are located. ICS has been a leader in instructional teleconference services since 1965. Its experienced staff is committed to service, high-quality, and innovative services to meet the needs of today's learners.

If you're looking for "more than tips," you'll want to access the URLs we provide throughout the book, as well as the stories our instructors tell about their effective practices. The URLs and stories are noted at appropriate places throughout the tips. We hope they enhance your learning experience. Enjoy!

FOREWORD

At Instructional Communications Systems (ICS), we work with synchronous and blended technologies on a regular basis, providing both instructional design and technical support. Along the way our Instructional Design Team has developed and acquired countless tips that have proven to be extremely valuable in their work with our distance education clients.

The tips selected for this book are based on years of experience and grounded in distance education research. Rosemary Lehman and Rich Berg have placed these tips in the meaningful framework of the instructional design process: Pre-planning, Planning, Developing, Implementing, and Evaluating.

Whatever your distance education responsibility—administrator, instructor, instructional designer, graphics designer, web designer, site coordinator, technical personnel, resource support, or evaluator—we know that you will find this book to be both practical and valuable. Whatever your level of expertise, whether you are only a beginner in the field of distance education or are someone who is very experienced, we are confident that this book will greatly increase your chances of success.

Tips are, of course, only bits of information that you can easily remember and call to mind when you need them most. They are just the "tip of the iceberg," so to speak. More in-depth information lies beneath. For that reason, we've developed a companion web site that will provide you with more in-depth resource material, references, and examples. The URLs for this web site are integrated throughout the book.

These tips are certainly not "all inclusive." You may have tips that you've used in your distance education experiences that haven't been included here, and you may discover new ones as you embark on or continue your distance education journey. We'd like to invite you to share those tips. For this purpose, the authors have created a blog. A hyperlink to the blog can be found on the publisher's web site and on the *147 Tips* companion web site.

Special thanks to the authors, Rosemary Lehman and Rich Berg, who are sharing their experiences with you, and to recently retired Bruce Dewey, who was a critical part of their team. Very special thanks to everyone they have worked with over the years, their "tip partners." They are an integral part of this work. They all deserve our thanks for advancing the field of distance education and making our ongoing journey easier and richer.

Marcia Baird

Director, Instructional Communications Systems
University of Wisconsin-Extension

FIRST THOUGHTS

Companion Web Site:
http://www.uwex.edu/disted/training/pubs/147tips/first.htm

It's becoming more and more common to dismiss history and quickly "jump into the fray of the present," missing the value and richness of the context that the past provides. We do this at a great price, we think. It's a price we do not need to pay. A glance over our shoulder at what brought us to the point we're at will give us a stronger foundation for dealing with the rapidly changing world. We'd like to do that—to take a glance back...

A brief look at the history of distance education is both fascinating and surprising. Learning at a distance began more than 100 years ago, in the late 1800s with the advent of correspondence study, allowing people to learn at a distance anytime and anyplace—asynchronously. The University of Wisconsin was one of the pioneers in the correspondence study field. In fact, the term "distance education" was first defined in a University of Wisconsin catalog in 1892. Fourteen years later, university professors extended this type of learning to the use of "new media" as they began recording their lectures and sending records to their distant students for playing on phonographs. This was later followed by the integration of other types of distance learning—radio, television, and audio and videotapes.

Beginning in the 1960s, technologies for real-time synchronous learning that more closely simulated the face-to-face experience, were being created—two way interactive audio, and later live interactive satellite, webconferencing, videoconferencing in its many forms, and, more recently, webcasting, and instant messaging over the web, along with the continuously emerging mobile devices. While initially these synchronous technologies held great appeal for learning at a distance, the rapid growth of the Internet and the World Wide Web began to take over as the preferred way to teach and learn remotely. But, interestingly, as this asynchronous movement grew, an increasing number of teaching professionals began to sense that something was missing—being present in "real time," socializing and interacting, exchanging dialog formally and informally, and collaborating.

The growing sophistication and flexibility of synchronous technologies and continuing advances and familiarity with their use began to open up new opportunities for engaging students and relating with them socially. This sparked an interest in reexamining the full array of distance education technologies—asynchronous and synchronous—and the consideration and interest in ways the two types might be blended. There is an escalating realization that distance education offers more than only teaching and learning online.

Today we have an array of technologies from which to choose, mix, and match. Our choice need no longer be the use of only "one" technology. Rather, we can now select the technologies that work best for specific learning experiences, and blend them.

Why Synchronous Technologies?

The question that must be foremost in our minds when we begin to plan to teach or meet remotely is, "What can best be accomplished asynchronously and what in real time?" Debra is an English teacher who has been asked to teach her traditional classroom Creative Writing course to four remote locations. Her course, which includes extensive reading and research, is based on students looking at pictures, feeling what the pictures have to say, and then writing stories about them. Once the stories are written, students share them by reading them aloud and explaining how the story evolved. Collaborative stories are then created by dividing the students into small groups, following a group process, writing the stories, and sharing them in much the same way. Toward the end of the course a collection of the stories is published in paperback form, an event is created to promote the book, and a celebration is scheduled.

After analyzing her course, Debra decided that she would use live, two-way interactive videoconferencing. The features of that particular technology allowed for:

- seeing faces and facial expressions
- hearing voices and voice nuance
- immediate visual and verbal feedback
- immediate support from the instructor and class
- instantaneous collaboration
- real-time socialization

It seemed to be the ideal technology—but, she asked herself, should all of the course be carried out in this way? Were there areas of the course that could be better taught in other ways?

Why Blended Technologies?

Debra thought about all of her course materials that might be posted to a course web site, and about posting the syllabus to the site, as well. She also thought about her need, and the need of all of the students, to get to know each other before the class started, not leaving that to the first videoconference session. To accomplish that she could have the students fill out profiles on the web site and upload pictures. She would do that as well. She could also use the web to test the students' writing before and after the course: a pre- and post-test. Guest authors had always been a part of her traditional classroom course; she could bring them in via audio (cost-effective) and have their picture on the document camera. Finally, what about one face-to-face event for the final celebration? The remote sites were all within the state. This would be a possibility. It became obvious to Debra, as she thought her course through, that one technology doesn't fit all situations. Various technologies could be blended and face-to-face incorporated as well.

Blending technologies helps to:

- better fulfill specific needs
- create course or meeting efficiency
- provide flexibility
- appeal to different situations, content, and learning styles

Educational organizations, governmental agencies, non-profit groups, and businesses all profit when they learn about the potential and limitations of asynchronous and synchronous technologies, how to ask the right questions in selecting them, and how to blend them.

Selecting Technologies—Twelve Questions to Ask

1. Why do we need technology and what do we want to use it for?
2. How can we best reach our audiences?
3. When will we need technology—anytime, in real time, or both?
4. What is the potential for interaction/collaboration—anytime, in real time, or both?
5. What technology features do we need?
6. How can we ensure accessibility?
7. How can we best meet the needs of diversity?
8. Will the learning curve be high or low?
9. What instructional design help is required?
10. What will we need for additional space and support?
11. What will the contribution of the technology be to the organization?
12. Will what is selected be cost effective?

A Little Theory

Whatever you decide in using synchronous and blended technologies, it's essential to ground what you do in theory. Our research and work with synchronous and blended technologies are based on the theory of *perceptual systems*. Past distance education theories have looked at technology from delivery and industrial viewpoints. Our viewpoint is a human one and is learner-centered. It takes the dynamic learner into consideration and also respects emotion as an essential component of cognition and behavior. It sees technologies as valuable tools that, thoughtfully selected, used, and blended, can help effectively shape the learning experience. It assumes that we are all, instructor and learner alike, active participants in the world around us. Whether teaching or learning informally or formally, it acknowledges that it is critical to (1) pre-plan, (2) plan, (3) develop, (4) implement, and (5) evaluate. These five areas form a framework that helps guide us as we design learning experiences for the world around us, and for the virtual world of distance education.

With this framework in mind, ICS has developed a useful videoconferencing book that also applies to the use of other technologies and the blending of technologies, *The Essential Videoconferencing Guide: 7 Keys to Success* (Lehman 2001). In this learner-centered guide, the critical areas are understanding the learner, knowing the environment, being a team player, developing formats and strategies, creating interaction activities, integrating support, and monitoring for quality. For more information see:

http://www.uwex.edu/disted/training/pubs/147tips/sevenkeys.htm

What's the Difference?

Teaching and learning at a distance are different from teaching and learning in the traditional classroom and it's helpful to think about it in those terms. Visualize and think about the classroom with four walls and your experience of teaching and learning there. Now visualize and think about a virtual classroom with remote locations and the use of synchronous or blended technologies. Consider the differences that you will encounter in all of the teaching and learning areas you can imagine. What will you need to change, expand on, minimize, or rework? How will you need to accommodate to make the course or meeting work effectively? We hope that the "What's the Difference" chart will help stimulate your thinking. You can see it at:

http://www.uwex.edu/disted/training/pubs/147tips/whatdiff.htm
http://www.uwex.edu/disted/training/pubs/147tips/whatdiff.pdf

A Lot of Practice

When you learn a new sport, learn how to play a musical instrument, or to write, paint, or take photographs, it's essential that you learn as much as possible about that particular sport or art, develop your skills, implement what you develop, and then thoughtfully and critically practice, practice, practice. Working with synchronous and blended technologies is no different. The learning and integration process is the same and can't be accomplished without thoughtful and thorough practice, practice, practice...

PRE-PLANNING

"Before you plan—pre-plan."

Companion Web Site:

http://www.uwex.edu/disted/training/pubs/147tips/preplanning.htm

Introduction

During our distance education experiences at ICS, it has become evident that in designing for distance education, we are not merely involved with setting up a meeting, a course, a program, or a session, but rather, are involved in designing an overall experience in which participants can personally encounter the learning event. This begins with the pre-planning process, a process in which you gain and solidify administrative support, gather information, learn more about yourself as an instructor, explore marketing options and registration logistics, and place your focus squarely on the learner and how you will engage the learner via the technology. In essence, you are laying a foundation for success.

1. Ensure administrative support before and throughout the course.

The full support of your organization's administration is essential. This should be obtained long before you begin planning, designing, and developing your course. Teaching at a distance requires more preparation time, particularly if you have never done it before. Find out what compensation is available at your institution. If none is offered, document research data to make your case for additional training, a lighter course load, release time, course assistance, or other type of compensation. Provide your administration staff members with regular reports about the progress of your course and invite them to observe a course session.

2. Read about synchronous/blended technologies.

There are many books and resources available that have been written about each of the major technologies. There are also many resources and books that discuss different strategies for using these technologies, how best to develop and implement them, and the effective practices that have resulted. Ask your technology coordinator or technology center about resources and books that they might have available. Read as much as you can for ideas and to formulate strategies for success.

One book that may be especially useful to you is *Using Distance Education Technology: Effective Practices* (Lehman, Dewey, and Berg 2002). This book contains 25 successful case studies that illustrate the use of various technologies in K–12 schools, higher education, state government, and non-profit organizations. The book also has a companion web site where new case studies are added as they are submitted. All of the case studies are authored by the people who actually developed courses and programs and taught via the technology. They discuss what they did, what worked—and, in some cases, what didn't. For more about this book see:

http://www.uwex.edu/disted/training/pubs/147tips/effective.htm

3. Talk to peers who have taught via the same technology and search the web.

One of the most valuable resources for you is peers or colleagues who have already taught using the same technology or blend of technologies. Ask them to describe their experiences to you. Solicit their advice about what worked for them and about the strategies they used to implement a successful experience for their students. Also ask them about the "lessons learned" and what they would do differently.

The web is another valuable resource. Do some web searching and look for online discussion groups or blogs that focus on teaching with technology. Talk to your school, campus, or district technology coordinator to see if there are other instructors who would be interested in forming a peer network to share ideas, strategies, and success stories. If you find experienced colleagues to work with you, ask them to join the network in an advisory role.

4. Secure the help of a distance education instructional designer/trainer.

If you are unfamiliar with teaching via distance education, securing the help of a distance education instructional designer or trainer will be a great help to you. The instructional designer/trainer should have formal training (certificate or degree) in designing materials for use in distance education and in teaching via technology. This person will help you think through your course, determine strategies for converting your present resources for use in distance education, and help you develop your materials.

Members of the Instructional Design team at ICS have both formal training and years of experience in developing and using instructional materials with a wide variety of distance education technologies. To learn more about personalized consulting from ICS, a unit of the Division of Broadcasting and Media Innovations, University of Wisconsin-Extension, visit:

http://www.uwex.edu/disted/training/pubs/147tips/ics_uwex.htm

5. Select the appropriate technology.

As you learn about and work with the various distance education technologies you have in your educational organization, you'll realize that some technologies are better-suited to your needs than others. Remember Debra's story on page 14? Selecting the appropriate technology or technologies for your specific needs is critical to the success of your course. In some cases, a blended technology approach may be the best solution.

Asking the right questions before you make your selections is the critical first step. Questions to start with are:

- Why do I want to use the technology?
- Do I want to use it anytime, in real time, or both?
- Do I want the students to hear me and each other?
- Do I want the students to see me and each other?
- What is the potential for interaction/collaboration—anytime, in real time, or both?
- Will my students need in-class time to collaborate on projects or assignments?

- What technology features do I want to use: PowerPoint®, electronic images, video, web search, simulations, collaboration tools?
- Will my students be using a discussion board, email, or other means of communicating with each other outside of the actual class time?
- How can I best meet the needs of diversity?
- How can I ensure accessibility for all of the students?
- Will the learning curve be high or low?
- What instructional design help is required?
- Will my choices be cost effective?

6. Self-reflect and examine your assumptions and philosophy.

Instructors come to the teaching experience with assumptions and a philosophy that impacts the way in which they design, develop, and teach their courses. If you have never taught via distance education before and have not examined your assumptions as they apply to distance education, you will certainly want to do this as you begin to think about the design of your course. For example, some faculty strongly believe that education should be delivered via lecture and that technology is just the means to deliver the information. They also believe that it is possible to take their classroom materials and use them "as is" when they teach via the technology and that class preparation will take no more time than for the traditional classroom. Those who have taught via technology know that this isn't the case. Teaching as though education is information to be delivered can be "deadly" for students. Students don't want to be receivers of information, but rather want to be engaged and to participate. Teaching to engage students also takes advantage of the interactive and visual characteristics of the various technologies.

7. Leave your comfort zone.

When you challenge your assumptions and philosophy and those of your students, you may need to explore unknown territories that are not completely safe or comfortable for you. This provides a growth experience for you as well as for your students. By challenging yourself, you shape new assumptions, reshape your philosophy, and become more open to innovative ideas and novel teaching/learning experiences.

In this new zone, your students can often be a great help to you. Those who have grown up in the world of technology have an intuitive sense about working with a variety of technologies. Don't be afraid to ask for their help when you need it. Although you are the instructor, they can often co-instruct with you in certain areas. Don't be uncomfortable with this new way of learning. Welcome it!

8. Let your personality shine through.

Teaching and learning via distance education technology is an experience that physically separates you from your students. But it need not actually do this. There are many ways to design your course, adapt your materials and teaching methods, and engage and work with your students so that your personality shines through and you feel as though you are all in a virtual classroom. With confidence, be who you uniquely are, incorporate your special sense of humor, and encourage your students to do the same. This is one of a number of things you can do to put students at ease and help the technology become more transparent. When students are at ease, it is easier for them to interact in ways that will be beneficial to them and to the other class members.

9. Highlight your strong points.

Just as you have certain characteristics that make you uneasy or take you out of your comfort zone, you also have characteristics that help you do things very well and with great ease. Reflect on your strengths and use these strengths for your benefit and the benefit of your students. Be willing to use these areas of strength to make the most of your sessions. Rely on your strengths and build on them. Be willing to take risks. A University of Wisconsin professor in the Department of Educational Administration took a risk when she decided to teach a graduate level course via videoconferencing, the web, and via videotape. At first a critical skeptic, she turned into an enthusiastic believer: Learn more about this study at:

http://www.uwex.edu/disted/training/pubs/147tips/strong_points.htm

10. Strengthen your limitations.

Just as everyone has strengths, they also have limitations and weaknesses. Take an inventory of ways in which you need to improve. One way to do this is to work with a designer to help you develop your materials and then to schedule time to practice your teaching via the technology. Have the technical staff record your teaching experience. Then either self-critique, or better yet, ask a colleague to view the recording with you and offer recommendations. Another suggestion is to have someone sit in on one or more sessions and provide you with feedback. In the synchronous environment, there are often characteristics that are amplified over the technology that we do not realize we have until we view them on a recording or have them pointed out to us by observers. I'll never forget watching myself on video prior to my first distance education experience. I had never realized that I was a "head-nodder." I certainly realized it after viewing the tape and have worked hard to change that habit.

11. Learn about presentation skills.

Teaching in the virtual environment can be more challenging than traditional face-to-face instruction. Facial expressions and body language may be non-existent if you are teaching via webconferencing without video. If you are teaching over videoconferencing you may be seeing your remote sites on a small screen. Both of these situations present you with challenges. Being mindful of yourself as an instrument and acquiring and practicing effective presentation skills for the virtual environment will benefit both you and your students. Learning, practicing, and using these skills will help you keep students engaged and interactive, and will enhance learning. These skills also apply when using webcasting.

For some pointers on presentation skills, access the presentation skills PowerPoint® slides at:

http://www.uwex.edu/disted/training/pubs/147tips/presentskills.htm
http://www.uwex.edu/disted/training/pubs/147tips/presentskills.pdf

12. Learn to be flexible.

Flexibility in the distance learning environment is a "must" and can become one of your most valuable assets when teaching your course. Because of the many variables in this environment, technology may hit a snag or activities may take more or less time than you imagined. When this happens, don't panic. If you've practiced and rehearsed well, have additional resources available, and have sent contingency plans to the remote sites, or if you can easily shorten or augment a module, you'll be able to breathe easily no matter what happens.

13. Change will help you grow in new directions.

Being an instructor in the distance education environment can be a catalyst for change. For example, your materials will need to be adapted to work with the potential and limitations of the technology that you're using. You will need to rethink your text and visual materials, your instructional methods, and other aspects of your course to be successful in the distance education environment. Think of this change as a challenge and an opportunity. Thinking through change often helps us become more aware of our assumptions and the ways in which we've taught in the past. Also consider taking advantage of professional development opportunities on change. By being open to change, you can explore new ideas and directions.

14. Learn to create a virtual presence.

In the traditional face-to-face classroom, students see you up close and personal and can instantly feel a connection. This feeling is harder to achieve in the distance education environment. Creating presence at a distance, however, is critical to the success of your synchronous and blended technology courses. Through the design of your course, your ease with teaching in this new way, your focus on all of the learners, your use of enthusiasm, emotion, and humor, you can give all of your students the feeling that you are actually in the room with them. This feeling, your virtual presence, will encourage students to interact with you and others in a natural way. Two articles that discuss virtual presence can be found at:

http://www.uwex.edu/disted/training/pubs/147tips/presence.htm
http://www.uwex.edu/disted/training/pubs/147tips/presence_long.htm

15. Market your course.

People might not sign up for a virtual course if a traditional course is being offered at the same time. Another factor is that people who are interested in taking your course may simply not be aware that it's being offered. When your course has been developed and accepted by your institution, make certain that it is listed on the institutional web site. A well-designed web page that gives a thorough description of your course and the technology that will be used will help prospective students decide if the course is right for them. You may also consider a small ad in the school online newspaper, or posting fliers on your campus. A limited postcard mailing can also "get out the news" to those who might not otherwise know about your course. For example, if you're leading a course about updating teaching credentials for K–8 teachers, you may want to send informational postcards to K–8 administrators to generate interest. Whatever the form, your marketing should be informative and stress the positive aspects of your course:

- learning a new technology that may be useful in the future
- early morning, daytime, or evening hours
- meeting other learners from across the state, nation, or globe
- meeting educational requirements
- the ability to attend class from home or the office, if this is the case
- cost savings
- other benefits specific to your course

16. Simplify registration.

One of the most frustrating aspects of taking distance education courses is difficulty with the registration process. If students have a hard time registering for your course, they may decide not to take it, or they may start the course with a feeling of resentment and anger. Make certain that the registration for your course is easy to understand and clearly explained. Students also need to have very specific information answered for them as they register. For example:

- Is the course only being offered at non-traditional times?
- Is there the need to travel to a special site to use a special technology?
- Is there a need for a high-speed Internet connection, or a newer computer?
- What about additional resources that are needed?
- Are there any additional costs?

17. Focus on the learners, not the technology.

You may find the technology very exciting to work with, but a word of caution, don't let the technology be the focus of your course. The technology is a means for helping you reach out to your students and should be as transparent as possible. Your students and learning are the focus of the course. (You might want to review the section on A Little Theory on page 16). The technology allows you to teach to others who may not be able to take the course in any other way. Also be careful about overusing the "bells and whistles." Often they distract rather than enhance your course. Always ask yourself how anything you decide to use will help the learners in your course realize the course objectives.

PLANNING

"Failing to plan is planning to fail."

Companion Web Site:
http://www.uwex.edu/disted/training/pubs/147tips/planning.htm

Introduction

Once you've laid your foundation for success by thoroughly pre-planning, it's time to begin the actual planning process for your specific course, program, or session. This involves finding out about your learners and their needs, learning about the various site locations and technologies, and beginning to orient yourself to the new distance education environment. As you become more familiar with this environment, it will be important for you to begin to visualize what teaching in this environment will be like. Orienting yourself through familiarity and practice and developing a similar orientation for your students is a "must." Bringing your students into a virtual classroom and creating a sense of presence is indeed a challenge. There are tips for making it happen, and when it does happen it's an incredible feeling. The technology seems to melt away.

18. Understanding learners is essential.

Teaching and learning are human processes, based on the assumption that we are all active participants in the world around us. From this perspective, understanding learners is central, whether in traditional, asynchronous, synchronous, or blended settings. Finding out about and understanding learner needs, characteristics, and expectations helps provide a solid framework for designing and developing course sessions, selecting and organizing resources, building rapport, and developing a sense of community. During the past several decades, there has been an astonishing growth of non-traditional learners with increasingly diverse needs. Many of these learners are more mature and are active participants in the world of work. They bring a wealth of experience and specific expectations to the learning experience, along with diverse needs and a strong motivation to collaborate in their learning process and help create meaningful experiences. It is imperative that we understand our learners.

19. Think learner-centered and perceptual learning.

Research during the past decade refutes the idea that learning is merely access to information and bears out the importance of a learner-centered approach (Gibson 1998). This method assumes that the learner is an active participant in the learning process and learning experience. Critical theories have been developed that focus on cognitive, constructivist, and interactive approaches. More recently, research on the perceptual nature of learners has expanded these approaches and looks at the significance of the dynamic interplay of learners with the environment, between their private world and their shared world. This approach is embedded in the enactive perceptual process (Lehman 2003, 2006; Noe 2005). From this viewpoint, obtaining learner profile information, student characteristics, uniqueness, educational needs, expectations, cultural background, and previous experience; ensuring relevance; considering learning styles; and accommodating special needs becomes critical. For citation information, see:

http://www.uwex.edu/disted/training/pubs/147tips/learner_centered.htm

20. Ask learners to fill out a profile.

One way to better understand learners is to ask for information from them prior to the beginning of the first class session. Profiles provide a framework for acquiring this information. Information that you would ask for in this format might include: name, organization, city/state, phone, email, fax, previous experience with the course content, reasons for and interest in taking the course, hobbies, interests, and any special needs. As the instructor, you should fill out an information profile, as well. Your profile will differ somewhat and should include: name, official title, department, educational history, membership in professional organizations, publication history, professional awards, honors, hobbies and interests, email, phone, fax, office hours and location. Learning Management Systems (LMS) also have profile components that can be used.

21. Ask for pictures of learners, pets, or hobbies.

"A picture is worth a thousand words." Ask your students to add their photos to their profiles. This will help you visualize your students before the first session starts. Occasionally, students will hesitate to add their photo. This may happen for a variety of reasons (shyness, reasons of privacy, or security). Honor their wishes and ask them to instead provide a photo of a pet or a hobby. This will provide important visual information for you as well, and give you additional insight into their personalities. And don't forget to add your photo—or that of a pet or hobby—to the written information you've provided in your profile.

22. Ask about learner characteristics.

For more in-depth information about those you'll be teaching, ask about distinguishing characteristics and uniqueness. This might be included in the profile or it might be a separate short paragraph that the students will share with you and others later when the class starts. Distinguishing characteristics are qualities that help define a person. Uniqueness is the quality of being "one of a kind"—that singularity which distinguishes a person from all of his or her counterparts. Providing time for the students to reflect on their distinguishing characteristics and uniqueness and express their thoughts will help them become more self-aware and help you, the instructor, in designing the course and advising the students.

23. Ask about learner needs.

Learner needs depend on what learners hope to realize from the course and how they plan to apply what they've learned. Their needs will encompass cognitive, emotional, and psychomotor components, as well as a blend of these three areas. To meet learner needs, reflect on what you've learned about them and provide flexible course design, with options for diverse learning styles and preferences, taking into account experience, cultural differences, and special needs. You'll also want to provide opportunities to move beyond shallow thinking to critical thinking, deep processing of information, emotional awareness, and collaborative and social learning. Psychomotor learning ensures both skill and information retention. Offering what is right for your students, will better prepare them to select what is needed for them individually, develop strong relationships, and move forward with their learning.

24. Ask about learner expectations of the course.

For some students your synchronous or blended course may be the first one they've taken. They may not know what to expect. Clarifying expectations prior to the first class session will help alleviate student misunderstandings. Your expectations will be clearly indicated in your syllabus and course instructions. But what expectations do students bring with them? For example, if your course will be via videoconferencing, do they expect to watch the class as they would a television program, or have you clearly said that the course will be interactive and that they will be class participants? If you will be using webconferencing, do they understand that this is a very interactive technology when tool and sharing permission is granted to them? If you are using webcasting, are they clear that this is more of a broadcasting tool and less interactive? Are they aware of the amount of time they will need to spend on the course? Most students juggle work and family with their courses and knowing what to expect for time commitment is very important.

25. Ask about level of learner expertise.

No doubt, your class will be composed of learners with varying degrees of expertise and experience. The profile, survey, and pre-test will help you identify the levels you will need to plan for in content and activities. Varying levels of student expertise can work to your advantage. They can provide a valuable opportunity for organizing group work. Individuals with varying levels of expertise and experience within a group can learn from each other. This also provides the prospect of setting up mentorships, a concept that is gaining in importance. Those with more expertise and at more advanced content level can help mentor the novices.

26. Provide options and choices.

Providing options and choices is one of the best ways to address the diversity of needs and expertise that you are likely to encounter in your virtual classroom. Using the profiles and the characteristics-sharing, as well as the pre-tests, chart the spectrum of expertise levels in the class. Looking at that spectrum, develop options and choices that will appeal to these levels. In addition, create collaborative group work situations that will mix these levels and enable those in the group to lead, follow, and learn from each other.

27. Ask about special needs.

With the Americans with Disabilities Act (ADA) and other government regulations enabling increased access for people with special needs, it is essential that instructors and staff explore ways in which to accommodate these needs. In the case of synchronous technologies, this may mean adapting materials for use with a "screen reader" for students who are blind or sight-impaired. It may mean either captioning videos for deaf and hard-of-hearing students or providing interpreters or audio transcripts. It may mean ensuring that there is wheelchair accessibility and appropriate furniture for wheelchair-bound students or instructors. With the extensive use of the web for blending technologies, it is critical to comply with the Section 508 standards and guidelines. The training courses we've taught have included all of these situations. In addition, we are always careful to develop our web sites to meet the Section 508 guidelines. For information about the ADA Policy, 508 Guidelines, and other valuable special needs web sites, go to:

http://www.uwex.edu/disted/training/pubs/147tips/ada_policy.htm

28. Test for learning styles.

Another type of diversity that needs to be addressed is learning styles. Howard Gardner's research on multiple intelligences (1993) has opened our eyes to the multiple lenses through which each of us views reality and learns from it. While it may "seem" that we are seeing and using information in the same way, that isn't the case. Understanding and testing for these intelligences will help you design your course for the variety of learning styles in your class. Helpful tools are the Multiple Intelligences Survey (http://surfaquarium.com/MI/inventory.htm), the Myers-Briggs Type Indicator (http://www.knowyourtype.com/mbti. html), and the David Kolb Learning Style Inventory (http://www. algonquin college.com/edtech/gened/styles.html). The Multiple Intelligences Survey helps students identify which intelligences they excel in and where their weaknesses lie. The Myers-Briggs tool focuses on personality types, while the Kolb inventory emphasizes perception and processing. This information can be used later during the course, by having students reflect on what they've discovered and build on their findings through first identifying their assumptions and then clarifying them through journaling and sharing. For citations, see:

http://www.uwex.edu/disted/training/pubs/147tips/test_learning_styles.htm

29. Find out about cultural backgrounds.

How fortunate we are that the majority of our classes are increasingly including students from a wide variety of cultural backgrounds, different races, ethnic backgrounds, religions, political viewpoints, and family composition. With your students' approval, find out about cultural differences and ask them if they would like to include this information in their profiles. Rich cultural diversity brings together varying perspectives and points of view that would be impossible to experience in an homogenous setting. Where this rich cultural diversity doesn't exist, it is possible, through the use of blended technologies, to create a shared cultural experience. Two Wisconsin K–12 schools have done so for years, and continue to do so, through innovative uses of technology, arts projects, and face-to-face. See:

http://www.uwex.edu/disted/training/pubs/147tips/cultural.htm

30. Determine international considerations.

When connecting with synchronous and blended technologies, you may be connecting to countries and cultures that were not a possibility when you taught within the four walls of a traditional classroom. Connecting with remote sites internationally "in real time" means that you will need to take into consideration time zone differences when scheduling. You will also need to make a concerted effort to understand other languages, dialects, and accents. In addition, reading resources on cultural etiquette should be a "must" for both teacher and students. One excellent resource is Harris, Moran, and Moran (2004). For citation information, see:

http://www.uwex.edu/disted/training/pubs/147tips/determine.htm

31. Decide on other essential information.

Finally ask yourself, "What have I forgotten? What else might be important to know about my students to help me better understand them and design and implement the course?" Additional areas might include obtaining more information about the remote locations that the students will be learning from and about any outside responsibilities that they would like to share with you—and determining ways to help them cope with these issues.

32. Help learners create a virtual presence.

The virtual classroom lacks the cues of presence that we are so familiar with in the traditional classroom. You thought about your virtual presence as an instructor (Tip 14, page 25), and about how you can adjust for this new and different teaching/learning experience. How can you help your students create a virtual presence with you and with others in the class? How does this differ using the various synchronous and blended tools? You might want to have your students review the two articles referenced in Tip 14. They can be found at:

http://www.uwex.edu/disted/training/pubs/147tips/virtual_presence.htm
http://www.uwex.edu/disted/training/pubs/147tips/presence_long.htm

33. Develop a class roster.

Now that you've laid the groundwork for understanding your learners, it's essential to develop your class roster. This roster will be a great help for easily identifying your students during the first weeks of your distance education class. With videoconferencing and webconferencing your students will be at multiple sites. Divide the roster into a diagram of site locations and have the diagram in front of you during your classes. Write information cues that you've gleaned from the profile, survey, and pre-test next to each name to help you better visualize each student as you meet them synchronously. As you call on each student and as each student participates, check his or her name and make notes. This makes it easier to remember students and to identify those who have not participated in class interaction. You can then encourage those who haven't participated to be more interactive.

34. Explore the origination site's physical environment.

Familiarize yourself with the physical environment of the site you will be teaching from. Look at the room configuration, ask what the seating capacity is, know where all of the equipment is located, understand the capabilities of the cameras, computer, other ancillary equipment, light switches, electric blind controls, and the help desk phone. Also be mindful of the location of restrooms, drinking fountains, vending machines, and tech support offices. If your technical person is not able to stay with you for your entire session, make certain that you obtain a phone number you can call in case of an emergency.

35. Find out about the remote sites.

Visit each of your remote sites if possible. If this is not possible, work with site coordinators and technical staff to find out more about each site. Ask about the room configuration, placement of equipment, seating capacity, the technology that is available, and parking for students. Think about how those sites are different from yours so that you can visualize them when your course starts. During the first session of your course, ask the students to take you on a camera tour of the room (if videoconferencing) and an audio description (if webconferencing).

36. Assure that all sites are accessible.

All sites should be accessible to all students in your course. Some of your students may have special needs. You will have to find out about wheelchair ramps, elevators, wheelchair accessible doorways and restrooms, adequate space for guide animals, adequate space and lighting for sign language interpreters, and assistive listening devices. If you know that a student with special needs will be attending at your site or another site, be certain to work with the site coordinator and other staff to ensure that the site is truly accessible.

37. Be mindful of the appearance of all sites.

The appearance of the sites will have an effect on how students perceive the use of the technology and the course. Encourage local building staff to repair or replace broken furniture and cabinetry. Encourage them to take care of peeling paint, worn carpet or cracked flooring, stained or broken ceiling tiles, dirty or cracked windows, "spaghetti" wiring, and anything else that detracts from the appearance of the site.

If the rooms are not configured properly for your particular course, talk to technical staff about a reconfiguration. If the rooms are poorly lit, find out about additional lighting. If there is no site identification sign, ask about the possibility of obtaining one.

Examples of well-designed distance education rooms can be found at:

http://www.uwex.edu/disted/training/pubs/147tips/appearance.htm

38. Avoid room clutter at each site.

Room clutter can be a distraction to the instructor and to learners, both at the origination site and at the remote sites. Work with students, site coordinators, and technical staff to reduce clutter by removing unnecessary equipment, furniture, boxes, and other items. If you are using videoconferencing, getting rid of clutter can also aid in setting up camera shots that will be aesthetically pleasing and not distracting. Wall clutter is another thing to keep in mind. When you set up camera shots, make certain that unnecessary posters, pictures, etc. have been removed. In addition, try to avoid switch or plug plates in your shots.

39. Avoid any distractions.

Take care to prevent any unnecessary distractions. In addition to the distraction of room clutter, ask students to turn off their cell phones and put away iPod®s and other equipment that might interrupt the class session. Also, remind students to mute their microphones when not addressing the class to prevent any unnecessary noise coming from their site. Post a sign on the classroom door letting people know that you are in a "live" distance learning session and should not be interrupted.

40. Ensure proper lighting in all areas of the room.

Improper lighting can be a major problem with videoconferencing, webconferencing with video, or webcasting. Too much light will tend to wash out skin tones and encourage closed eyes or excessive blinking. It can also increase the heat in the room. Low light, on the other hand, will leave subtle facial expressions and body language lost in shadow. If necessary, contact technical or room set-up staff to work out a lighting solution. For effective lighting, keep in mind photo lighting: back, spot, and fill.

41. Collaborate for optimum console/desk arrangements.

Work with technical staff and building personnel to arrange your teaching room in the best possible configuration for your purposes. Due to wiring and receptacle constraints, this may be a major undertaking.

Make these requests as early as possible to allow adequate lead time. Never rearrange wired/cabled equipment without prior approval from your site contact and/or tech staff.

42. Arrange for appropriate equipment components.

At times you may need technology components that are not part of the regular setup for your site. These may include a VCR, DVD player, document camera, laptop computer, or other component. Check with your site contact to make sure that such a component is available and that it can be installed in your room. These requests should be made as early in the course as possible to give tech staff adequate lead time. Also check to see if there will be any additional charges for using such equipment. If your students will be presenting from remote sites, work with their site personnel staff to ensure they have what they need and that everything is conveniently located.

43. Ensure that the technology is well-maintained.

Technology that doesn't function properly or doesn't work at all will make it difficult for you to make the most of your possibilities. This requires testing your technology ahead of time. If you find something broken or working improperly, report it to the proper person. If it is not fixed or replaced within a reasonable amount of time, find out if there is a way to expedite the process. If there is not a way to speed things up, develop alternate plans to deliver your content in ways that will still be engaging and foster interaction.

44. All sites should be equal.

Nothing is more discouraging to learners than to feel that they are less valued than others. Work with the site coordinators at all of your sites to ensure that each site has equipment comparable to your location and that all students can participate fully. This will enable students to use the same tools that the origination site will be using. Give all of your sites equal attention. Remember that your course classroom is a virtual classroom in which you are trying to bring everyone together on equal terms.

45. Develop a site and contact list.

It is important to know who to contact when there is a problem at a site. Having a site list and contact list will help you to find the right person at the right place in a short matter of time. The list should include the names, titles, and contact information of the department head, site coordinators, and technical staff, as well as the Help Desk. Make certain that a copy of the site and contact list is sent to all of the site locations.

46. Test all visuals and technology features.

To avoid lost class time, test all the visuals and technology features that you intend to use well in advance of your scheduled class time. By testing well in advance, you will have adequate time to fix or change visuals and to find other technology applications that will fit your needs. It is also a good idea to test your visuals and slides across sites. Monitors are often calibrated differently. The color you see at your site may look quite different at the remote sites.

47. Practice, practice, practice!

Nothing will prepare you for a successful session like practice. You should not only practice your presentation or lesson, but also practice with the different technologies that you will be using. Practicing your presentation will help to find any flaws that may exist. Practicing with the technology will help you to feel more comfortable, making it easier for you to present your material, thus projecting an image of confidence to your learners. Remember the analogy in the introduction about learning to play golf or a musical instrument? Practice, practice, practice is essential!

48. Provide a technology orientation for students.

To ensure that students at all sites can actively participate in the class, it is important that they learn how to use all of the equipment properly. Students who are unsure of how equipment works will be less likely to participate in the class.

In webconferencing, make certain that students know how to use the participation tools, if you have decided to share them. In videoconferencing, a sample orientation would include having the students work with the controls of the room cameras, document camera, and other equipment, as needed. The students should work the camera controls individually, with the site coordinator being able to answer questions and lend assistance, if necessary. Have the students set up wide and close-up shots using both the audience and presenter cameras. Also have them practice working with the document camera, and switching between different cameras and the document camera. A sample orientation can be found at:

http://www.uwex.edu/disted/training/pubs/147tips/orientation.htm

49. Personal considerations: Ensure student comfort.

Students who are uncomfortable will have a harder time staying with your course sessions. Make sure that heating and cooling are adequate, that there is enough seating, that the room is not cramped, and that visuals are large enough for all students to see without straining. Also, if your class is more that one hour long, plan for short breaks that will allow students to stretch, use the restroom, and acquire refreshments.

50. Set the tone during the first session.

Be prompt and on time and orient the students to the technology environment. Let the learners know exactly what is expected of them. Lay out guidelines for attendance, class behavior, assignment deadlines, and any other area that you feel necessary. Providing learners with a positive beginning and clear-cut expectations will help to eliminate confusion and prevent problems later in the course.

51. Use learned skills to create presence and a virtual room.

Remember Tip 14 and the articles we referred to? Review these tips again and also the articles. Establish a sense of presence by welcoming all students to the course and personalizing by calling them by name. Start off with an icebreaker that will stimulate participation across sites. Use your learned presentation skills of looking directly into the camera when addressing the far sites, dividing your attention equally among all sites, speaking in a natural tone of voice, incorporating humor, and letting your enthusiasm and personality emerge. If you have students at your site location, as well as at remote sites, you will need to divide your attention between the students at your location and the ones at the remote sites.

An excellent example of accomplishing virtual presence can be found in the article, "International Videoconferencing Media Literacy Forum," in which one of the participants said, "We began in separate rooms miles apart and by the end of the day, the walls disappeared and I felt as if we were in one room." See:

http://www.uwex.edu/disted/training/pubs/147tips/skills.htm

52. Plan, plan, plan!

This section started with the statement, "failing to plan is planning to fail." This applies in all areas of our lives and certainly applies in the area of creating, developing, and implementing courses and programs. Successful courses and programs are the result of sound planning. Planning is particularly important in the distance education environment. Lack of planning fails to consider the many variables that can have an effect on what you hope to accomplish. An essential framework for planning is the development of a detailed timeline that provides you with the opportunity to look at the "big picture" and the many component parts and variables that need to be considered as you move along the timeline. It ensures that everything necessary has been considered and will be completed on time. It is absolutely critical to plan, plan, plan! ... and use a timeline for the process. An excellent sample of a well-planned training seminar is the Jury Bailiff Training. Extensive planning and thoughtful design resulted in an award-winning session that is now archived for continuous self-paced training. A full article can be found at:

http://www.uwex.edu/disted/training/pubs/147tips/plan.htm

DEVELOPING

"Developing is a gradual unfolding, making the plan visible."

Companion Web Site:
http://www.uwex.edu/disted/training/pubs/147tips/developing.htm

Introduction

The centerpiece for your development process is the development of a detailed timeline, and the communication process you will use to track your progress and keep in touch with everyone who will be carrying out the various functions of the sessions you will be teaching. Organizing your course according to objectives/outcomes, scope and sequence, individual chunked sessions, and maximum engagement; developing your materials appropriately for the various technologies and component print pieces; thinking visually and interactively; and acquiring necessary copyright clearance and release forms will increase your chances for success. And remember to always have a Plan B, in case Murphy decides to pay you a visit!

53. Develop a detailed timeline.

The development of a detailed timeline begins with deciding on the date of your course or program and then backtracking to determine when you need to start to accomplish all of the necessary details—selecting remote locations (if necessary) and dates; identifying team members; planning and producing all course materials; clearing copyright; training for use of equipment or software; sending welcome and registration information; learning about and communicating with participants; developing your profile; receiving the student profiles; and orienting students to the technology or software. An example of a timeline can be found at:

http://www.uwex.edu/disted/training/pubs/147tips/timeline.htm

http://www.uwex.edu/disted/training/pubs/147tips/timeline.pdf

54. Begin communications with team/contacts.

Instructing via synchronous and blended technologies is never a "one person" endeavor. It involves working with a team of people who will help ensure success. Depending on the simplicity or complexity of the sessions being planned, the size of your team will vary. In most cases it will not be a team that you will need to construct, but personnel who are already available in your and other participating institutions. It will be your responsibility to contact them, negotiate ways in which they can best help you in your course, agree on and clarify roles and responsibilities, and network and communicate with them on a regular basis. Your team/contacts may include administrative personnel, instructional designers, graphic designers, technology personnel, site coordinators or learning liaisons, and resource personnel. Your early and regular communication with these team members will help ensure success.

55. Define team functions.

One way to make certain that you have all responsibilities covered is to create a functions chart. The chart will help you visualize the function areas that need to be covered. Look at your list of team members and decide who will fill each function. If your course is simple in design and your team list is short, members may have to wear many hats and carry out several functions. If the course is more complex and you have the people resources, you may need a person for each role under the functions.

Refer to your timeline and list all of the functions that need to be covered. A sample functions chart can be found at:

http://www.uwex.edu/disted/training/pubs/147tips/function.htm

http://www.uwex.edu/disted/training/pubs/147tips/function.pdf

56. Define roles/responsibilities with each team player.

Looking at the necessary functions and defining roles and responsibilities at the outset will eliminate confusion. Once the roles have been identified, clearly outline each role's responsibilities. Be certain that you share each of the roles and responsibilities with all of the team members. If there is overlap, as there well may be, clarify the overlap, ensuring that all team members are in agreement. Doing this will provide a solid base for a strong and amiable working relationship and enhance the important concept of being a team player. Next, chart the responsibilities and send the complete chart to all of the team members. A sample roles/responsibilities chart can be found at:

http://www.uwex.edu/disted/training/pubs/147tips/rolechart.htm
http://www.uwex.edu/disted/training/pubs/147tips/rolechart.pdf

Now refer to your roles and responsibilities chart to make certain that all functions have been covered. If not, communicate with your team members and revise the chart.

57. Train team players in necessary areas.

While the majority of your team members will be professionals who have been trained in their area of expertise, some may need training in the technology or blend of technologies that you will be using. For example, in videoconferencing or webconferencing site coordinators may have other responsibilities in their regular position that either have not included distance education in the past or only include it periodically. Or, your instructional designer may be very competent in designing for the web, but may have had little experience with synchronous technologies. Survey your team to find out what technologies they have worked with in the past. Coordinate the necessary training for those who need it far enough in advance so that they will be able to use the skills as they carry on their roles and responsibilities.

58. Ensure that equipment and software is tested before the first session.

Many distance education courses or programs have started out on a low note because essential testing hasn't taken place. In the case of online web work, the Learning Management System (LMS) software and registration process should be as error-free as possible. This can only be accomplished through early testing and retesting. If this important area is neglected, students will become confused and frustrated at the beginning of the course and may decide to opt for another course. In addition to testing the equipment and software, schedule or post an orientation for the students to ensure that they know the registration process and the various components of the LMS. In the case of videoconferencing and webconferencing, test all sites with the technical personnel who will be doing the bridging. As with the online LMS, orient the students to the technology.

59. Ensure that the remote bridging is tested.

When more than two remote sites are used with synchronous and blended technologies, a bridge to connect the remote sites is necessary. In the past, bridges could connect only one type of technology. For example, an audio bridge was used for audioconferencing and a video bridge for videoconferencing. Bridges in use now can connect multiple types of technologies and multiple variations of the types. With videoconferencing, for instance, integrated services digital network (ISDN), fiber optic, and Internet technologies can all be connected for a course on the same bridge. In addition, audioconferencing and webconferencing can be added to the mix. In every case, it is essential to test connections to each of the sites prior to the first course or program session.

60. Communicate, communicate, communicate!

Just as we've emphasized "practice, practice, practice" and "plan, plan, plan," we need to emphasize "communicate, communicate, communicate!" We've previously noted the importance of communication in Tip 54 on communicating with team members and other contacts. Clear and regular communication can resolve a multitude of problems. Use the team/contacts chart to set up an overall listserv and sub-listservs for various individual groups you'll be communicating with: the technology group, instructional group, support group, and others. And don't just rely on email. Think about using Instant Messenger (IM) and the phone. Each type of communication has its own unique characteristics. Think about which method works best for your purposes.

61. Be prepared and well organized for your part as instructor.

Teaching via distance education synchronous and blended technologies requires that an instructor be prepared, well organized, and flexible. For more in-depth information on this subject see the article on instructor characteristics (Lehman 2000) at:

http://www.uwex.edu/disted/training/pubs/147tips/instructor_success.htm

In this teaching and learning environment just "winging it" will not work. Make certain that you are well-trained in the use of each of the technologies that you will be using—that you know the limitations and potential of each technology. But that's only the first step in the process. Make certain that you have worked with each technology, created your course with the various technologies in mind, and that you have set up several rehearsals. Rehearsing is essential. Working with multiple technologies takes skill, flexibility, practice, and rehearsal, just as in learning to play golf or learning to play a musical instrument.

62. Create advance information for registration.

Sending out advance information for course registration is an essential step in securing students for your course and a component of the marketing that was discussed in Tip 15. This information will let potential students know about your course content and process, the days and times the course will be held, any necessary prerequisites, and any special equipment that they might need—for example, a laptop, MP3 player, or scientific calculator. Post this information to your school or department bulletin boards, and to your web site. Also consider other areas where students would be likely to see course information. For example, you may consider placing an ad in the school's electronic newsletter. If your course will have multiple campus participants, work with the people in the remote locations to publicize the course to these students. The more students know about the course, the more likely they are to register for it.

63. Prepare a welcome letter.

Once students have registered, send a welcome letter to each one or post it on your web site or in your LMS. A welcome letter to each student personalizes the course and gives you the opportunity to let students know exactly what to expect from your sessions. Be straightforward with your students about what you will be expecting and provide them with all necessary information for the course. Develop a format for your letter and send the identical information to all of your students. You may choose, however, to write the student's name at the opening of each letter and sign each letter by hand for an even more personal touch. You can use an electronic signature for the web version of your letter. You can find a sample welcome letter at:

http://www.uwex.edu/disted/training/pubs/147tips/welcome.htm

64. Develop a detailed syllabus.

Just as in the traditional face-to-face course, a detailed syllabus is a must. This should include information on course number; instructor's name and contact information; the title of the course; credits for the course; course description; all assignments; the teaching methods you will be integrating; details about the technologies being used; course objectives; all instructional materials; course requirements with all dates, times, and locations for the sessions and assignment due dates; a course outline; all course readings and resources (divided for individual sessions) and when they are to be read/viewed; criteria for assignment grading; the grading point system you will be using; and office hours. For a sample blended technology syllabus, see:

http://www.uwex.edu/disted/training/pubs/147tips/syllabus.htm

http://www.uwex.edu/disted/training/pubs/147tips/syllabus.pdf

65. Provide an instructor profile or bio.

The nature of distance learning makes it more difficult for your students to get to know you as well as they would in the traditional classroom. You most likely will not have met before the course starts and are only a name to them. By providing them with your professional and personal information prior to the course as suggested in Tip 20, you can help them through the "getting to know you" process. There are several options. You can develop a profile on your course web site or LMS or you can create a bio-sheet and distribute it to your students. Whatever you decide to do, it should include your name, title, educational background; teaching experience; book, journal, article, or electronic publishing; awards; and hobbies. You should also include a recent picture. A sample profile and a sample bio sheet can be found at:

http://www.uwex.edu/disted/training/pubs/147tips/instr_bio.htm

http://www.uwex.edu/disted/training/pubs/147tips/instr_bio.pdf

66. Determine your method for office hours.

When teaching synchronously at a distance, finding the right method for office hours can be a challenge. It will be impractical for most students to come to campus, since one of the reasons for taking the course at a distance is that they prefer not to travel. First, determine all of the communications options you have for conducting office hours.

Next, check on the availability of any equipment/rooms you will need. Also check the availability at the remote sites. You can now set some initial times for your office hours. Then, ask your students if they will be available to meet during the days/times you have provided. You may need to be somewhat flexible and adjust the days and/or times for a few in the class. Try to stay with whatever you have set up, but be willing to accommodate students who have legitimate reasons for needing the change.

67. Decide on what is public and what is private.

You may want to make some of your course materials available to the general public, while keeping other materials behind a secure web site or LMS, especially those that are your intellectual property or are covered by copyright or copyright agreements. Determine what you want or are willing to let become public and what you want to keep private within the course. Protect the private materials by storing them in a password protected environment, and by letting students know that these materials should not be shared with others outside of the course.

Privacy also applies to student information. Work with your students to have them decide if there is information about them or materials that they have developed that they would like to keep private.

68. Develop course guidelines.

Another phrase that we think of often as we design and develop for distance learning is, "Manage or be managed." Without well thought out structure, it is very easy for your course process to become confusing, and we all know that confusion hinders learning. To manage your course well, develop clearly established guidelines and include them in the syllabus. Guidelines should include rules for using the technology, being on time and attending all sessions, behaving respectfully, completing assignments, meeting deadlines, and the consequences associated with not adhering to the guidelines. To assist you, check to see if your school or institution has guidelines that are already established and that you are required to follow as part of policy. Also, colleagues who taught via synchronous and blended technologies in the past may be able to offer you a template or some tips in setting up your guidelines.

69. Develop online tutorials as necessary.

In some cases, your students may need certain skills that you've had little time to cover in class or during office hours. In this instance, the development of online tutorials can be very helpful. If done well, they will require minimal instruction from you. When creating these tutorials, you should make certain that they are written in an easy-to-understand style. Be certain to include as many pictures or screen shots as necessary to relay the major points. If you have time, you might also consider using a program that allows you to capture actions on your screen and make an animated tutorial for your students. Finally, develop your tutorials in both HTML and PDF. While a web page may work for some, others need to hold the instructions in their hand. The PDF lets them print it out in the original format. For a sample tutorial see:

http://www.uwex.edu/disted/training/pubs/147tips/tutorial.htm
http://www.uwex.edu/disted/training/pubs/147tips/tutorial.pdf

70. Work with an instructional designer for program design.

If you are new to developing materials for this environment, you will need the help of an instructional designer. Work with this designer to assist you in understanding the potential and limitations of the technology you'll be using and to help you with the development of your course and the materials associated with it. An instructional designer can help you overcome many of the challenges and issues that are common when changing from the traditional classroom to the distance education environment. As you become more accustomed to this new way of teaching and learning, you may feel more comfortable designing your course and course materials, and rely less on your instructional designer. In addition to consulting an instructional designer, it is very helpful to talk to colleagues who have taught via the technology that you'll be using. They'll have important "lessons learned" to share with you.

71. Develop instructor and learner protocols.

Protocols are rules of conduct and behavior. Inherent in protocols is consideration and respect for others. They help you, as the instructor, manage and facilitate your course so that it runs smoothly, and they help your students understand how to work most effectively in the distance education environment and how to relate to others. We recommend developing a protocol for the instructor and a separate one for your students. The instructor protocol will provide guidelines for you to manage and move your course forward. The student protocol will assist students in understanding what is expected of them during the course sessions, how they should interact with you and other students both during the live sessions and outside of the live sessions. Protocols should be short lists of what to do to realize the most effective course sessions. Protocol lists should be posted on the course web site and can also be incorporated into the syllabus. You should also "talk through them" during the course orientation to the technology. Sample protocols can be found at:

http://www.uwex.edu/disted/training/pubs/147tips/st_protocol.htm

http://www.uwex.edu/disted/training/pubs/147tips/instr_protocol.htm

72. Consider your overall content, goals, and objectives/outcomes.

While designing for synchronous and blended technologies has some fundamentals that are identical to teaching in the traditional classroom, there are also many differences. The overall framework, for example, does look quite similar: (1) define the learning goals, the learning situation, and identify your learners; (2) determine your objectives and assessment approaches; (3) create your materials, activities, and projects; (4) plan how to integrate feedback; and (5) develop formative and summative evaluations. At this point, however, other areas that apply specifically to the synchronous and blended technologies environment need to be taken into consideration: (1) determining the scope and sequence of your sessions and deciding on which technologies will be most effective for specific parts of your course, (2) deciding on the composition of your team, (3) developing a timeline to guarantee continuous communication and ensure that everything will be accomplished for the course's start date, and (4) thinking visually and interactively to design a program with short modules or chunks of information that will engage your students and meet learner needs.

73. Develop content scope and sequence.

The design of your synchronous and blended technology course depends on a flexible set of criteria to reference during the design process. (1) What desired outcomes, knowledge, and behaviors do you expect? (2) What content needs to be conveyed to meet the needs and achieve outcomes? (3) Overall, what sequence or order of content is necessary for effective learning via the technology? (4) Within each session, what sequence or order is necessary? (5) What special opportunities does synchronous technology permit that would not exist in the classroom? (6) What visuals, interactive techniques, and media are needed to achieve the program goals and what roles will they play? (7) How will you measure the effectiveness of learning in this new environment?

Answering these questions will help you determine your course scope, the number of sessions, the objectives for each session, how the material will be sequenced, what visual and interaction activities will enhance the course, and how you will determine if the objectives have been met.

74. Determine individual sessions and chunk into modules.

Students will stay engaged in the course and learn more effectively if the course content is thoughtfully divided into individual sessions and if the content within each session is chunked into discrete learning units of information that vary every 10 to 15 minutes. This process of dividing and chunking allows learners to more easily grasp individual concepts, ideas, and facts before relating them to other knowledge that they have acquired or will acquire in the course. Chunking content into small units of information also makes it easier to develop homework assignments, activities, projects, vocabulary sets, and quizzes, because you will able to focus on smaller areas of your content matter instead of your course as a whole. This process also helps to hold student attention and engage them actively in their learning. An example of chunking can be found at:

http://www.uwex.edu/disted/training/pubs/147tips/chunking.htm
http://www.uwex.edu/disted/training/pubs/147tips/chunking.pdf

75. Think visually with your content.

Throughout the design process, it's important to think visually. If you have an instructional designer and graphic designer on your team, they will work closely to guide you through this process. If they are not a part of your team, the following questions are important ones to ask: (1) How do I envision the program as a whole? (2) How do I envision each session? (3) How can the various visual tools help me convey my message? (4) Will text work best or do I need an image or text/image combination? (5) If I choose an image, will a still visual work or should it be an object, a moving image, or an actual simulation?

76. Think interactively with your content.

As you design your course, it's also essential to think interactively. Again, an instructional designer can help you here. When there is no instructional designer, ask yourself these questions: (1) Where within the course is interaction appropriate? (2) What types of interaction activities will best meet the needs of your students? (3) How will the interaction activities need to be adapted for use via the technology? (4) What materials will be needed to carry them out effectively?

77. Consider the six types of interaction.

As you design your interaction activities, consider the various types of interaction. We have identified at least six types for the distance education learning experience that build on Moore's (1989) three types of interaction: (1) instructor to learner, where the instructor starts the interaction with the student; (2) learner to instructor, where the student begins the interaction with the instructor; (3) learner to learner, where the learner interacts with other learners in the class or course; (4) learner to content, where the learner interacts with the course content; (5) learner to medium, where the learner interacts with the method of delivery (videoconferencing, webconferencing, or webcasting); and (6) learner to context, where the learner interacts with people who are not in the course, like co-workers or family members. To view a diagram detailing the six types of leaner interaction and the citation for Moore's three types of interaction see:

http://www.uwex.edu/disted/training/pubs/147tips/interaction.htm
http://www.uwex.edu/disted/training/pubs/147tips/interaction.pdf

78. Develop individual experiences.

Learners need to feel that they are not just another name on the course roster. Whenever possible, allow students to personalize the information and to contribute to the course with their own stories and accounts. Maybe they have taken a unique approach to solving a problem that you have posed, based on a previous life experience. Perhaps they have developed a mnemonic device based on a song by their favorite singer. Or, they may have come across some relevant course information that others haven't seen. Encourage these types of experiences and build on them. Any personalization that contributes to the course can be a way for learners to feel that they have ownership in the course and encourages them to succeed.

79. Develop group experiences.

As important as the individual experience is, it is also important to develop group experiences within and outside of the course setting. Group experiences include discussions, problem solving, activities, and projects. When creating and developing group situations, try changing the members from time to time. In this way, students will have the chance to interact with a wider number of students in their course. In addition, different types of groups offer different types of learning experiences and provide learners with a wider variety of perspectives. Try to be creative in setting up the groups according to: (1) specific interests, (2) levels of expertise, and (3) depth of experience. It is also valuable to mix interests, levels of expertise, and depth of experience. The choice is yours, depending on what you think is important for the specific group activity.

80. Create ongoing learning experiences.

Ongoing learning experiences can continue throughout the semester or the year. While you may create learning experiences that will only last for a short period of time, you can also create ongoing learning experiences for your students by having them work together on investigations like the changes in the local ecosystem during the year or semester-long reading groups. In ongoing learning experiences new information builds upon old information that has already been acquired to provide a learning process that is a continual flow throughout the semester or year. In addition, these experiences help the virtual classroom interface with the real world.

81. Select appropriate interaction activities thoughtfully.

As you've learned by now, interaction is one of the key components to the success of your course. This does not mean, however, that all interaction activities are useful or valid in your class situation. You must select and develop them thoughtfully and always ask if the activity is appropriate for the specific situation. Choose activities that will not only provide interaction, but will also have strong instructional grounding and contribute to enhanced student learning. We have created an Interactivity Spectrum Chart that has been very helpful in our training sessions and is widely used by those we have worked with. You can view the Interactivity Spectrum Chart and interactivity descriptions at:

http://www.uwex.edu/disted/training/pubs/147tips/spectrum.htm
http://www.uwex.edu/disted/training/pubs/147tips/spectrum.pdf

82. Develop effective visuals and graphics.

Your visuals and graphics should enhance the course content that you are covering. Visuals and graphics should be detailed enough to provide sufficient information for student understanding, but not contain so much detail that the students will be distracted by superfluous information. There are required rules to follow, which are dependent on the medium that you will be using for your visuals and graphics. For more detailed information about making effective visuals and graphics go to:

http://www.uwex.edu/disted/training/pubs/147tips/visuals.htm
http://www.uwex.edu/disted/training/pubs/147tips/visuals.pdf

83. Consider other media and tools.

Synchronous technologies can interface with a range of media and tools. Often the base technology you're using may not have the features for conveying the point you are trying to make. In this instance, consider using additional media like movie clips, guest speakers brought in via audio, audio CDs, computer animations, the web, and other tools that will enhance your course sessions. These media and tools should never be integrated just for "flash" or effect, but should have a definite, direct instructional value that is designed for the unit or area that you are teaching. A media tools chart that will be helpful to you can be found at:

http://www.uwex.edu/disted/training/pubs/147tips/media.htm
http://www.uwex.edu/disted/training/pubs/147tips/media.pdf

84. Develop appropriate print materials.

Print materials complement the course sessions that you've developed for your students. They can take the form of brochures and posters to announce the course; they can be developed to provide more depth and enhance the materials you are using in the course sessions; and they can take the form of workbooks, manuals, supplementary handouts, etc. These printed materials can also be posted to the web or the course LMS. Whatever is developed should be specifically designed for the course you're teaching, include easy-to-understand instructions, follow established instructional design guidelines for print materials, and have the look and feel of the web and session materials designed for the course.

85. Become familiar with copyright law.

With multiple materials in your course, it is likely that you will need to deal with copyright. All copyright should be dealt with "up front" rather than "after the fact." Contact the legal department at your organization to become familiar with how your institution is handling copyright. Also consult reliable sources in your library to find out more about copyright law and how it will apply to you and your course. Knowing more about copyright law will help you gain a clearer understanding of what you can use in your course and what kind of permissions and releases you will need to obtain.

86. Become familiar with fair use law.

Often questions arise about copyright use in distance education as to whether or not copyrighted materials will fall under fair use. The debate has not yet been settled and is still a grey area. Our response to the questions we receive is, "If in doubt, do!" If there is any question in your mind or in the mind of those who work with copyright issues in your organization, make certain that you obtain clearance for all the copyrighted material that you use in class or post to your course web site. Also, make certain that your students understand this as well, since their actions with copyrighted materials may have an effect on you and your organization.

Classroom agreements are usually not broad enough to cover telecommunications transmission, videotape recording, or the distribution of course related materials. While the Copyright Act permits "fair use" and non-profit exemption for the purpose of teaching in the classroom, its application to telecommunications requires legal analysis that can often lead to cloudy answers. If you are unsure of this, you should talk with your campus legal staff to find out what the current fair use laws are. Check back periodically to see if there are any new laws, or suggest that your institution establish a web site for posting and updating this information.

87. Develop a copyright audit list.

Once you become familiar with copyright and fair use law, you will want to ensure that you have covered all of the necessary materials in your course. A valuable way to ensure that all items are covered is to create a list of all the materials (books, articles, videos, movies, pictures, graphics, etc.) you are planning to use. Review all of the items for copyright clearance need and list all of the copyrighted works that will require clearance. Go over the list with your legal department, librarian, or other institutional source to find out what they will be able to clear and what you will need to pursue further.

88. Acquire copyright clearance.

The key to obtaining copyright clearance is to start early and have a backup plan. If you wait too long, you may not be able to obtain the clearance in time, and if you have no backup plan, you will not have any additional materials to furnish to your class.

To obtain copyright clearance, first work with your school or organizational librarians, as noted above. They are a wealth of experience in this area. They can provide you with the most recent policies and can also help you obtain the actual clearance. Another way to obtain copyright clearance is to contact the Copyright Clearance Center. They provide rapid response at very low costs. You can access their information at:

http://www.uwex.edu/disted/training/pubs/147tips/copyright_clearance.htm

Another group, Creative Commons, offers an alternative to full copyright clearance through a license agreement. Creative Commons information is at:

http://creativecommons.org

89. Be aware of trademark acknowledgment.

Trademark acknowledgment is another area in which your organization's legal department or your librarian can be helpful. Note any areas in which you will need to insert trademark symbols and contact or meet with your sources to go over them. Under federal law, you must acknowledge any trademarks that you use as part of your print, course session, or web materials. There may also be state laws that govern your use of trademarked materials as part of your course. If you plan to teach your course internationally, you will also need to comply with any international trademark laws that apply.

90. Develop contributor release forms.

In the process of obtaining copyright clearance and asking for permission, create release forms for all of the copyright items. While obtaining these permissions and collecting the release forms, you may want to consider asking for permission for future sessions of the course that you will be teaching. Your legal department can assist you in drafting these release forms.

91. Develop on-camera release forms.

If your students will be on camera during the course or if their images will be used in print materials, they should be fully protected by "on-camera" release forms. These forms must be signed by the students, or by the student's guardian, if the student is under age. They are then returned to the instructor. Many institutions are now requiring that the release form be included as a required part of the registration process for the course. A sample on-camera release form can be found at:

http://www.uwex.edu/disted/training/pubs/147tips/release.htm
http://www.uwex.edu/disted/training/pubs/147tips/release.pdf

92. Develop contingency plans for various situations.

No matter how well you plan, practice, and manage your course, there are so many variables in the distance learning environment that Murphy may make a visit when you least expect it. There may be instances of equipment failure, power loss, evacuations for fire, dangerous weather, or the illness of an important guest expert. If you are unprepared it will be very difficult to gain control of your class. By developing a number of appropriate contingency plans and having them readily available to site coordinators, along with detailed instructions, you can ensure that students are kept occupied until the situation has been resolved.

Develop general or specific contingency plans, using multiple scenarios that will work well with your particular group of students. You can view a sample contingency plan at:

http://www.uwex.edu/disted/training/pubs/147tips/contingency.htm
http://www.uwex.edu/disted/training/pubs/147tips/contingency.pdf

IMPLEMENTING

"Manage or be managed."

Companion Web Site:
http://www.uwex.edu/disted/training/pubs/147tips/implementing.htm

Introduction

Now it's time to think about implementing your sessions. Take comfort in the fact that you've done your pre-planning, planning, and developing. As you continue to practice for your sessions, think about balancing the structure you've developed with spontaneity, setting the stage for success and using our many tips for making things run smoothly. Focus on engaging the learners and creating a sense of community. Continue your contacts with all of those who are supporting your course and carrying out the various class functions. Ensure special needs support.

93. Ensure structure, but allow for spontaneity.

Structure helps your course run smoothly. Too much structure, however, can make your class seem stiff and boring to the students. A mantra to repeat to yourself is to "be flexible within the structure." Retain enough structure in your course so that students have a sense of order and progression, but also allow enough room to be spontaneous and capture the "teaching/learning moments" that often arise unexpectedly. Maybe there was an article in today's newspaper that relates to the subject matter in your course. Take time from the designed course activities to discuss the article and what it means to the subject matter you have been studying. Engage the students in responding in various ways both during the class and with new interaction activities. If a student brings up an interesting example that can be expanded upon, go with it and re-adjust the course and materials accordingly.

94. Set the stage for success.

The first few minutes of your first session are critical ones. They create the environment and set the tone for the sessions that will follow. Check the room background. Blue or peach tones work well for video technology. Check the equipment. Is everything ready? Be mindful of the lighting—set it for back, spot, and fill to produce clarity, depth, and dimension. Check the audio and any other media that you will be using. Ask the remote sites to follow this same process. Are you ready? With video, avoid wearing white, red, plaids, large designs, or pinstripes. They tend to distract, as does dangling/shiny jewelry. Avoid wearing the same color as the background or you will appear to be "one" with the background. Not a good idea. Check for clutter and place appropriate objects in aesthetic balance.

95. Frame camera shots for video or still pictures.

If using video, frame and set your camera shots. Framing is an art. Think about what you would like to convey to your learners visually and how you would like to appear to them at the remote locations. A closeup shot is a good one for conveying mini-lecture information. A mid-shot is better for conversation and interaction. It places you on a par with the learners. A far-shot will distance you from the students. A shot that looks down on you places you in a submissive position. One that looks up at you places your students in a submissive position and you in a dominate one. A straight-on shot at eye level works best; it enhances the all-important eye contact. Most keypads in videoconferencing let you pre-set a number of shots of the instructor and also of the students in your room.

Shots should also be framed aesthetically. Watch framing shots on television to model individual and group shots. Public television provides a particularly good example to follow. Notice the space on the sides of your shot and also the amount of space above the head. A rule of thumb is to place the eyes 2/3 up within the frame. Share this information with the technical personnel at the remote sites for their pre-sets. For framing examples, see:

http://www.uwex.edu/disted/training/pubs/147tips/framing.htm

http://www.uwex.edu/disted/training/pubs/147tips/framing.pdf

96. Ensure that audio is level at all sites.

Audio is critical in videoconferencing and webconferencing. Ensure that technical staff have leveled the audio for all sites so that everyone can be heard equally. When speaking into the microphones, you should be at an 18-inch to 24-inch distance. Talking into the mic too closely will distort the sound. Also, avoid moving the microphone around or rustling papers near it. These distracting sounds will be greatly amplified at the remote sites. If wearing a lapel mic, be sure to turn it off when you leave the classroom. Not doing so has resulted in some embarrassing situations.

Other annoying situations are audio buzz, audio echoing, and audio feedback. Work closely with your technical staff to trouble shoot these situations so that you can avoid them.

97. Use learned presentation skills.

If you are using videoconferencing, webconferencing, or webcasting, your course participants will spend a great deal of time watching you and listening to you. Remember that your presentation skills will be magnified through the lens of the camera and through the microphone. Learn about presentation skills and practice them. (Review Tip 11 on Presentation Skills.) It's always a good idea to practice your presentation skills with a pilot audience for feedback and critique, or tape yourself while you're presenting and watch the tape for self-critique.

98. Maintain your energy level.

From our experience and that of those we've worked with, we've discovered that it takes more real-time energy to teach over synchronous technologies than teaching in a classroom or online. The amount of energy needed is increased because of the concentration you will use in attending to remote learners, balancing between remote learners and learners at your origination site, and in creating the dynamic learning experience. This applies to both visual and vocal energy. When your energy drags, you will begin to distance yourself from your students and appear to be less present for them. Focus, engage your students, and try to be in the moment with them, transcending the technology.

99. Use your learned listening skills.

Listening is a skill that we often neglect. When teaching over synchronous and blended technologies it becomes critical. Watch and listen carefully to pick up the style and idea cues of your students. Take note of participant responses that you can refer to as the class progresses. When it's appropriate, paraphrase what someone has said to make certain that others have heard and understood what was said. Listen carefully to who is doing the most speaking and who is doing the least so that you can make an effort to encourage those who are not contributing to the class. A visually useful way to do this is to place a check mark on the class roster when someone has spoken. When you notice a student without checks, call on that person to encourage participation. It might be helpful for you to look back again at Tip 11 on Presentation Skills.

100. Balance eye contact between local and remote learners.

Often you will teach a synchronous class with students in your room as well as at the remote sites. This presents a challenge. While you need to focus on eye contact at the remote sites, you don't want to do this to the detriment of the students in your room. By the same token, you don't want to just focus on the students in your room and forget about those at the remote site. To counteract this, you'll need to balance your attention. Focusing on the remote sites at times and the in-room students at other times. Once you practice this, you'll notice that you can pace yourself and orchestrate it quite well. But, as with everything, it takes planning and practice. There are those words again—planning and practice. They are critical!

101. Utilize your voice as an instrument.

Because we use our voice on a daily basis to communicate, often in very casual ways, we take it for granted and forget that it is truly a wonderful instrument. It conveys our personality, our enthusiasm, and our confidence. We can vary it with inflection, expression, and pacing. We can vary it with pitch to add interest and stress critical points. And we can not use it—to good purpose. Silence can be golden when used effectively. We can pause to draw attention, we can create silence for reflection. The use of your instrument is both science and art. Use it well and use it aesthetically. Remind your students to be mindful of this as well.

102. Minimize gestures and repetitive behaviors.

All of us have certain mannerisms or habits that when viewed through the small frame of videoconferencing or webcasting, can be very distracting. Remember what I discovered in Tip 10, that I was a "head-nodder?" When I first saw myself on television, I realized that I had the habit of nodding my head very often. It took a great deal of concentration to stop "my habit," but with practice, I did. If you're working with videoconferencing or webcasting, watch yourself, note your distracting habits and develop a plan to minimize your overextending gestures and repetitive behaviors. It's amazing how unaware we are of our habits, until we see them within the small frame of the screen. Suddenly they become very apparent.

103. Start on time and end on time.

Always start your sessions on time and end them on time. If your sessions are scheduled to start via a computerized system, this is particularly important. In this situation, you have only a tightly scheduled amount of time and you want to make certain that you are using it well. Toward the end of a course that is scheduled via a computer system, be sure to end before signoff time. This will ensure that you will have time to finish everything you want to finish and to complete your last statement. Instructors who haven't followed this advice have been cut off mid-sentence. In a system that is scheduled manually, you will have some leeway. But even in this situation, starting and ending on time is a good policy for you and for your students.

104. Manage your time effectively.

Remember the phrase "manage or be managed" that we noted previously? We think of this often in the synchronous and blended technologies experiences. If you don't manage well, all of the variables in the distance education environment will manage you. This is true in all instances in the management of your time. Use the technology that you have selected in the most effective way. Design your materials so that you are using the potential of each technology. With the use of each technology, allot a certain amount of time for each teaching module or informational chunk that you will be teaching. Keep an eye on the clock, but remain flexible for those wonderful teachable moments. Be alert to adapting your materials/time when you feel you need to. Be careful and alert to the time and space you're working with.

105. Ask learners to turn off cell phones, pagers, and mobile devices.

Nothing is more annoying than "unintended interruptions" during a synchronous learning session. Remember to mute your mics unless asking or answering a question or making a comment. Cell phones and pagers are often the culprits. As an item in your protocol, note that all cell phones and pagers should be turned off prior to the session. It is possible that someone may need to be on call for an emergency of some sort. If someone is expecting an emergency call, they can use vibration in place of sound.

106. Personalize from the beginning.

When using synchronous and blended technologies, the technologies naturally tend to separate the instructor from the students and the students from each other. One of the ways to overcome this separation and create a more personal learning experience is to integrate personalization. Prior to your course, you've learned as much as possible about each of your students, their individual backgrounds, unique characteristics, interests, and commonalities with others who are registered for the course. Incorporate stimulating personalizing techniques into your course whenever possible to ensure that each student is being recognized. For example, call students by name, capitalize on their special interests and talents, send personal emails, develop ways in which they can share their talents and interests with others. These techniques will help to keep and maintain high attention levels.

107. Facilitate site-by-site introductions.

In most instances, your learners will not have met each other prior to your first session. You may have shared web site student profiles with all of your students, but they may not have seen faces or heard voices.

For this reason, it's very important to rotate sites at the beginning of the first session and have each person introduce themselves, the location that they are at, and tell something about themselves that they've selected from their profile information. This also immediately launches them into the interactive potential of synchronous technologies and models the way in which they will be interacting throughout the course. In addition, as instructor you can make use of the seating chart you developed for calling on students and tracking dialog. It's helpful to know that students do tend to stay in the same seats they've selected for their first class session. You can also request that they use the same seats until you become familiar with their names and faces.

108. Follow your instructor protocol.

Closely follow the instructor protocol that you've developed for your course. Some of the key points previously mentioned in Tip 71 were: become very familiar with the equipment that you'll be using, practice your presentation skills so that you are prepared and comfortable for your sessions, make certain that students have become familiar with the equipment and that they know what you expect them to use for various activities, set guidelines to let students know what you expect of them during the sessions and if there are any special rules they will need to follow, maintain eye contact with the students, balance attention with in-class and remote site students, use participant names whenever possible, and encourage interaction and dialog.

109. Implement the student protocol.

It's also time to implement your student protocol. Remember in Tip 71 you thought about how learning at a distance using synchronous technologies placed new demands on the learner. Asking questions, participating in class, and taking notes are still necessary, as well as performing other activities typically associated with classroom instructions. But, in addition, students will need to adjust to the new learning environment and bring a more independent and self-motivated approach to their learning. Make sure that students have a copy of the student protocol and that you have included it in the syllabus and also posted it on the web. Just to refresh you mind, students will need to be prompt and on time; in instances of more than two remote locations, mute their mics when not speaking; turn off cell phones and pagers; identify themselves and their location when they speak; make an attempt to stay focused; be proactive in asking questions of the instructor and engaging with students at the remote sites; restrict personal conversations during the presentation portions of the session; and find out about support services in the event that there is an equipment failure during the session. Implementing the student protocol that you've developed will assist the students during the course sessions.

110. Integrate interaction and visuals.

You now know that synchronous technologies are by nature both interactive and visual and you've learned to exploit these potentials. You've designed your course by thinking in parallel about interaction activities that were most appropriate for involving students within and across sites. You've also created activities that students might continue off-site or on the web. If you're trying something unique like role-playing, across-site debates, or inviting in guest experts, have them do some rehearsing before they actually execute the activity.

Visually, you've also thought in parallel about how the course will "look" to the students. The visuals you've created will enhance the learning experience. In addition, you may be asking your students to create PowerPoint® slides, bring in objects to display on the document camera, or show video or film clips. If you do, make certain that you've developed a tutorial for them. Also have them test the visuals first for clarity and sound and don't forget copyright clearance, if necessary. For a sample tutorial on how to create PowerPoint® slides, go to:

http://www.uwex.edu/disted/training/pubs/147tips/ppt_tutorial.htm

111. Allow for reflection opportunities.

In our fast-paced life, we rarely take time for an important component of learning—reflection. Don't neglect this. Reflection need only take a short period of time during your synchronous session, but the time spent is invaluable. One example of using this technique is during and after small group work. Following brainstorming, discussion, or planning ask students to spend a few minutes reflecting on either the process that was used or the small group topic. Individuals or groups can report back on the reflections. Other excellent tools for reflecting and documenting those reflections are journals, individual web sites, and, most recently, blogs. These tools are also a method for assessing what students have learned and the depth of their thinking.

112. Provide time for adequate breaks.

Sitting for long periods of time in synchronous learning environments can often be tiring and physically draining. For this reason, we suggest that students be given breaks every hour to hour and a half. Breaks and break durations can be varied in length and type. Ten- to 15-minute breaks are the typical ones that we think of, but there are other types of breaks that you can incorporate. For example, a short three-minute stretch break, a brief "breath of fresh air" break (if possible), or a two-minute "close your eyes" and relax break. Come up with your own creative suggestions. Breaks reenergize both you and your students.

113. Ensure that participants act responsibly.

When students are physically separated from the instructor and other students at remote sites, it is tempting for some of the students to become distracted, to lose focus of attention, and to "act up." For this reason, some universities, schools, and organizations have felt the need to develop student contracts. The student must agree to and sign this contract. In most cases, one breach is permitted. If a second one occurs, the person is not allowed to continue the synchronous course. The adoption of such a contract has greatly reduced behavior problems in the remote environments. This is especially true in the K–12 environment where remote locations are often not monitored by an in-room teacher. You can find a sample student contract at:

http://www.uwex.edu/disted/training/pubs/147tips/contract.htm
http://www.uwex.edu/disted/training/pubs/147tips/contract.pdf

114. Use learned skills to motivate learners.

Research indicates that motivation is an essential characteristic for learners-at-a-distance. Skills for self-motivation are critical in this environment and have a great deal to do with high self-esteem and a "positive success attitude." To become a self-motivator a number of fears need to be surmounted: the fear of (1) low self-confidence, (2) others being more qualified, (3) taking risks, (4) not being able to find the time, (5) others' high expectations of us, and (6) not knowing how to begin or how to continue. Instructors can use their learned skills for helping motivate students by helping them feel confident and able to conquer their fears. They can do this by first letting students know that it's alright to be frightened in a new environment. They can help them boost their self-confidence through the personalizing process, by clearly explaining the new environment and course expectations, by allowing time for the students to immerse themselves in the new technology and become acquainted with other course members, by developing small groups for support structure, and by developing flexible office hours and accessibility for dialog.

115. Draw on learner experiences.

Drawing on learner experiences will help your students in a number of ways. First, it will help students identify skills that they already have and may not have identified as strengths. Knowing about these strengths will help students build their self-esteem and build a sense of assurance for the course. It will also provide them with information that they can share with others. Through drawing on student experiences, the students will find others who share their experiences or want to find out more about them. Drawing on learner experiences will also help you, the instructor, be able to effectively match students for group work, special interests, project work, or mentoring.

116. Encourage learners to be proactive.

Many students think of synchronous technologies as ways to receive information, rather than ways to learn by participation. To break this mindset, instructors should, from the start, describe the technology as inherently interactive and the course as one of participation. This can be described on the course component web site, in information that is sent to the students, and in the course protocol. It will also become apparent through the development of your course formats and strategies that will include interaction activities. Throughout, students should be encouraged to be proactive in their questioning and activity participation. This type of learning environment greatly enriches the learning experience.

117. Use learned skills to create a sense of community.

In teaching via synchronous and blended technologies, the instructor should strive to create a sense of presence that will transcend the technology and bring all participants into one virtual room, creating a sense of community. There are a number of ways in which the instructor can accomplish this, among them: (1) let your personality shine through the technology by being comfortable in the synchronous environment and using your presentation skills, (2) personalize your course by getting to know your students and helping them get to know each other, (3) develop inter- and intra-site activities, and (4) create small and large group communication, activities, and projects.

118. Prepare guest experts for the new environment.

An instructor will often invite a guest expert to a synchronous course session to provide special information. This participation can take place via a phone call, with a picture of the expert on the document camera at the instructor's site or via another videoconference or webconference connection. More often than not, this guest expert may not have had previous experience presenting via a synchronous technology. It is highly recommended that a training session be set up with guest experts about a week prior to their participation in the course session. Some practical tips on their presentation skills, PowerPoint® slides, and process for Q&A will increase the value of the guest expert participation.

119. Continue contact with instructional design support.

If you've had the good fortune to work with instructional designers to help you learn about the technologies and adapt your materials for your course, don't sever connections with them when the materials have been completed. Keep in touch with these support personnel and ask them to review and critique your materials. If you are developing new materials, you may also ask them for suggestions. Learn from them and continue to practice good design principles with all of your materials.

120. Continue contact with training support.

As you continue to expand your use of new technology and media in your class, request additional training and refresher sessions. If the technologies at your site are changed or upgraded, you will need to request training for operating the new system or technology. Keeping in regular contact with the training support staff will make it easier for you to make appointments for training as needed, and will also help them remember to inform you of any changes that have been made.

121. Guarantee ongoing technical support at all sites.

Technical problems can disrupt class time and discourage students. Develop good, positive relations with the technical support staff at all of your sites. Let them know that you appreciate everything that they do for your course. Send them a thank-you note at the end of the course and mention that you're looking forward to working with them in the future. If you will be working with new sites, set up technical tests through your support personnel and make followup contacts with the technical support personnel at these sites.

122. Continue contact with graphics support.

You've already learned the basics of graphic design, but as you progress with your courses, you may want to become more sophisticated with your designs. Appropriate and well-designed graphics can boost class understanding and engage learners. Allow graphics support staff to critique graphics that you've designed and to provide instructions for improving them. In addition, attend workshops or mini-courses your graphics support group hosts on graphic design. Continue to consult with them as you develop new course graphics and ask them to update you as they become aware of new software and ideas.

123. Work closely with site coordinators for support.

Build on the rapport that you've developed with the site coordinators as you prepare for your course. They are critically important to your course's success. This is a very collaborative relationship. Make certain that you send all materials that will need duplication well in advance of the class date for which they are to be used. Let them know how much you appreciate their help and find out if there is anything that you can do to assist them. Acknowledge your appreciation with a thank-you note at the end of the course and let them know that you're looking forward to continuing to work with them in the future.

124. Work closely with resources support.

Course resources are an integral and critical part of your course. Work with your resource specialists to ensure that the resources you have selected are ready and available when you are ready to begin your course. If resources need to be ordered, plan well ahead of time so that resources are where you need them when you need them. If materials need to be sent prior to the beginning of the course for students to re-view, make certain that the resources support personnel are aware of this. A resources timeline should be an integral part of your overall time-line.

125. Ensure ongoing special needs support.

If you have special needs students in your class, you will want to have continued special needs support. Ask these students to evaluate your materials and class arrangements on a regular basis to see if they can help you find ways to improve them. This will ensure that you have pro-vided full and complete access for their needs and those of students that you will serving in the future. Keep in touch with the special needs of-fice at your organization and have them update you on new software and instructional methods. Another excellent idea is to ask special needs stu-dents whom you've had in your class to serve as consultants to you for future courses.

EVALUATING

"Refining and shaping the experience;
assessing learning effectiveness, and impact."

Companion Web Site:

http://www.uwex.edu/disted/training/pubs/147tips/evaluating.htm

Introduction

Evaluation is an integral part of the course design and needs to be considered up-front and written into the budget. It is not something that's tacked on at the end of a course. In our work with distance education we feel it's important to expand the concept of evaluation to include pre- and post-tests, formative evaluation, and feedback opportunities throughout the course. It's also essential to expand on the summative evaluation to include those areas in distance education that may have a very real impact on student learning: the site, the site coordinator, the technology, interaction activities, materials, and instructor's methods, etc. Together they'll help you determine how well your students have learned and if the course was effective.

126. Create a pre-test for expectations, experience, and knowledge level.

Evaluation should be designed upfront and worked into your budget. Pre- and post-tests are one component of evaluation. Pre-tests are used to determine the level of students' expectations, their experience, and their previous knowledge prior to taking your course. This method helps to collect baseline data that can be compared to outcomes in a post-test. Some questions to ask that apply to learning via technology are: What are the students expectations about learning via technology?

Have they taken a course via technology before? Do they know how to work with the basics of technology? If not, what will they need to know, and what will you need to do as instructor to orient them to this new type of environment? Create your pre-test to correlate with your post-test.

127. Create a post-test to measure changes from pre-test.

To evaluate the level of student improvement, a similar test or post-test should be created and administered at the end of the course or program. By comparing the pre-test to the post-test, valuable information about the student's improvement can be gained. When carefully and thoughtfully created, post-tests can be used to evaluate and validate what students have gained in the area of learning via technology. This method is an accurate and instant tool for measuring improvement. Sample pre- and post-tests can be found at:

http://www.uwex.edu/disted/training/pubs/147tips/pretest.htm

128. Explore feedback opportunities.

Feedback is an integral part of designing for synchronous and blended technologies. Feedback encourages change and modifies learning, the overall program, and is a continuous process. There are numerous opportunities for feedback during courses taught via technology. Feedback can come from the instructor during sessions as written or verbal feedback before, between, or at the end of the sessions. The site coordinator can also provide feedback about student involvement and protocol during and between sessions. Students can provide feedback to the instructor and also to each other. There are many opportunities for feedback during a course. You can find a sample feedback opportunities chart at:

http://www.uwex.edu/disted/training/pubs/147tips/feedback.htm
http://www.uwex.edu/disted/training/pubs/147tips/feedback.pdf

129. Develop and integrate activities for feedback.

To provide for continuous feedback during the course, create and integrate activities that provide for feedback. For example, at scheduled times during the course, the instructor could email the students and ask for their perceptions of the course. A framework of questions could include: Is the program time allotted via the technology adequate for the material being covered? Explain. Is the instructor encouraging participation from all locations? Is there enough time allotted for you to accomplish your assignments/projects? Is the instructor managing the sessions well? Is the course meeting your expectations? Comments? Is the instructor readily accessible for feedback? Do you have additional questions/comments?

130. Use feedback to reshape course.

An important use of feedback is the potential for reshaping the course to better align with the needs and expectations of the students. One university chemistry professor acquired feedback from his students that indicated they wanted more depth in the videoconferencing component of their blended course. To help answer their needs, he decided to add a new section to the course called "Where's the Beef?" During this segment he offered additional information and research that added more "meat" to the course. Student response to his change was immediate. They responded that they felt that he was being very attentive to their needs and that in addition to giving them more substantial information, it made them feel as though they were truly participating in the course.

131. Ensure immediate instructor feedback.

One of the most frustrating aspects of learning via a distance is that students often feel very disconnected from their instructor. When they send out a request for feedback and don't hear within a certain period of time, they begin to feel very much alone and at a loss as to where to go for the information they need. Instructors should provide a feedback section in their syllabus. This section should include all pertinent contact information and a designated time period during which the instructor will respond to feedback requests. Request responses should not go beyond a 24-hour time period. Some instructors set up electronic office hours within their LMS or via phone. Some hold office hours via video or webconferencing. The key point is that it be as immediate as possible and not exceed a 24-hour period.

132. Create questionnaires for survey responses.

Questionnaires in the form of a survey are an excellent way to have your students provide feedback. One health professor designed a survey called "Taking the Course Temperature." She used a rating scale of "Hot,

Lukewarm, Cool, and Cold." Then she asked the students to explain their responses and offer suggestions for "upping" the temperature. Another question she included was, "Do you see any severe weather ahead? If so, how are you planning to deal with it?" Still another asked them to forecast their success in the class and bullet-point how they planned to arrive at their success.

133. Create polls for quick response statistics.

Polls are an excellent way to receive quick responses from students. Often during synchronous webconferencing and webcasting courses, instructors create polls as part of their PowerPoint® slides to periodically test students on what they are learning or to gain additional information about how the session is going. In polls, as in email and survey feedback, the information can be used to shape the course. In the case of synchronous polls, the advantage is that it is instantaneous feedback and can be used by the instructor immediately.

134. Develop and implement your overall course evaluation.

The overall course evaluation for synchronous and blended technologies should be expanded to include those aspects of the course that are specific to the distance education experience. This is the comprehensive summative evaluation that is created at the beginning of the project, program, or course as part of the overall design and implemented at the end. It is a very valuable tool for evaluating all of the components of the course and pulling all of the information together for student input, final analysis, and a final report. It is an integral part of the program design process and includes questions about marketing, registration, the instructor, course development, site coordinators, delivery of the program, and additional questions. For an example of an overall course evaluation see:

http://www.uwex.edu/disted/training/pubs/147tips/exp_course_eval.htm
http://www.uwex.edu/disted/training/pubs/147tips/exp_course_eval.pdf

135. Evaluate learner progress in the course.

Evaluating learner progress in the course is the area of evaluation that instructors are most comfortable with. This is the type of evaluation that they have carried out in regular classroom sessions, so it should not present a problem. They should, however, remember that the new distance learning environment may have an effect on student progress. While some students take to it easily, others who are less motivated and need more structure and instructor guidance may tend to fall behind. The instructor must always be attentive to the reasons why some students appear to be not doing as well, increase their communication with those students, and offer them more intensive help and guidance.

136. Evaluate interaction during the course.

Course interaction can be evaluated in a variety of ways. Forms of course evaluation are no longer limited to the paper/essay, yes/no, or multiple-choice questions. New ideas for assessing individual and group interaction have evolved. Instructors can now choose from an array of either individual or group possibilities, using evaluations of their own creation or those of a growing number of evaluation software programs. These evaluations can be used to assess the six types of interaction previously noted that include discussion; journaling; producing audiotapes, videotapes, and podcasting; creating photo displays, projects, and simulations. Group evaluations can be assessed in the same way with the addition of using role play, drama, group discussion, and project work. Collections of interactions and projects then can be compiled into electronic portfolios for assessment. These suggestions are not all-inclusive, but can give you food for thought.

137. Evaluate course discussion.

In most cases you will have an online component with your synchronous technologies. This can take the form of a web site designed for your course that would include a discussion board, or an LMS with a discussion board. Specific questions can be posted to the board each week, with the requirement for two "thoughtful" responses to each of the questions. One of the responses can be to the instructor's question and another a response to another student's question. We provide specific instructions for online discussion. See course discussion guidelines at:

http://www.uwex.edu/disted/training/pubs/147tips/discuss.htm

Discussion via the synchronous technologies can also be tracked and become a part of the course grade.

138. Evaluate course projects.

Course projects provide an excellent means for helping evaluate student growth and progress. If the projects are relevant and apply to real-life situations for students, they will not only totally engage the students, but will also be a meaningful way in which they can apply the information they are learning in the course. Projects are becoming a common practice, particularly in courses with non-traditional learners who are often working and participating in distance education classes at the same time. Projects and student progress are increasingly being incorporated into student portfolios that they can add to during the progression of all of their courses.

139. Evaluate group collaboration.

It is also becoming more common to have students work in groups and collaborate on papers and projects. This is another way in which you can evaluate your students. One downside to this type of evaluation is that not all group members may pull their weight in the group. The result may give too high an evaluation to a student who has really been a slacker. If there are several slackers in the group it may even bring the group's grade down. Selecting a strong group leader and providing some guidelines for group responsibility will help create an environment in which you will be able to provide a more realistic grade.

140. Evaluate the course materials.

How many of you have asked your students to provide feedback on your course materials? In the traditional classroom, this is certainly not a common practice. In a course that deals with synchronous and blended technologies, this becomes very important. In this environment the instructor has adapted the course materials to take advantage of the potential of the technologies. Finding out how well this has been accomplished will be extremely valuable to instructors as they adapt and refine materials for future courses. These questions can be asked on an ongoing basis during the course via a questionnaire or survey and should also be included in the overall evaluation at the end of the course. Some questions to consider are: Is the content well formatted for the time available? Are the formats and strategies appropriately chunked to engage students? Are the interaction activities relevant to the course and are they well designed? Is the online course component clear and well organized? Are the print materials and visuals well designed and integrated?

141. Evaluate the site coordinators.

The site coordinator's evaluation is a relatively new type of evaluation that focuses on both the coordinator and the site environment. It is gaining in importance because of the potential for increasing the success of synchronous programs. The site coordinator's evaluation can be a part of ongoing feedback in the form of a questionnaire or survey and should also be a part of the overall evaluation at the end of the course. Questions might include: Did the site coordinator make you feel welcome? Did she/he communicate with you clearly? Was a positive atmosphere created? Was the site facility comfortable? Was it well equipped? Was it well arranged? Did the site facilitator have materials ready when they were designated? Did the site facilitator assist in facilitating interaction activities? Did she/he follow up on questions and concerns?

142. Evaluate the technology.

Evaluation of the technology used for the course is critical. In the ideal situation, technology should be transparent. Knowing that we do not live in an ideal world, we need to identify and troubleshoot any problems that arose during the course. This assessment should be a regular part of the ongoing feedback and also a part of the overall evaluation at the end of the course. You will want to know: Was there an adequate orientation to the use of the technology? Was the audio/visual quality clear? Were there any technical problems at the site? Were there any technical problems on the bridge? Was there an immediate response from the Help Desk? Was there followup on the problems? How were the problems resolved?

143. Evaluate the overall course design with team members.

At this point, it is extremely valuable to meet with your team members and reexamine the overall course design, refer to the student evaluations, the overall course evaluation, and the other evaluation components. Feedback from this meeting will help you refine next semester's team roles and responsibilities, the course content, interaction activities, and technical considerations.

144. Evaluate the instructor's methods.

Feedback on the instructor's presence and teaching methods can also provide critical information for refining the course for the future.

What does it mean to be present to your students during a distance education course? Identify what it means to create a sense of presence. What are the various ways in which you have accomplished this? Ask how you, as instructor, were able to break through the hard surface of the technology and appear to "be there" for your students. Did this involve your personality? The ways in which you used your capabilities as an instrument of expression? Your knowledge of the content? The manner in which you created the course? The feedback and followup during the course? A combination of the above?

For a sample presentation feedback, see:

http://www.uwex.edu/disted/training/pubs/147tips/present_feedback.htm

145. Evaluate the effectiveness of the course.

By combining information and data from the areas that have been noted above for evaluation and feedback, you will be able to determine the effectiveness of student learning and the effectiveness of the course. These include pre- and post-test, feedback through the various methods that have been employed, and the expanded course evaluation that includes student outcomes and progress, learning environment interaction during the course sessions and in online work, online discussions, projects, group collaboration, course materials, course delivery (technology and media quality), site coordinators, technical personnel, overall course design, and the methods and presence of the instructor. Taken together, these areas provide a comprehensive summary of the effectiveness of the course.

FINAL THOUGHTS

146. Relax and be yourself.

Remember Debra in our First Thoughts? Debra was once in the same boat you were in when you started reading this book. She knew very little about distance education teaching and learning. But she took a risk, did an exemplary job, and is still teaching via technology. You're on your way. Pat yourself on the back! You've just completed 145 of the 147 Practical Tips for Synchronous and Blended Technology Teaching and Learning. You've thought about selecting appropriate technologies for your work and you've gone through the process of thinking about pre-planning, planning, developing, implementing, and evaluating your course or program. You've looked at many component resources, read about colleagues who have already had the experience and have provided you with valuable effective practices and "lessons learned."

Now it's up to you to take the first steps toward making your course or program a reality. You can do it and, remember, we're here to help. One last word…

147. Enjoy!

Have fun! The world of synchronous and blended technologies for teaching and learning is an inevitable world and an exciting one—and you're on the cutting edge!

POSTSCRIPT

Developing and Designing for Emerging Technologies

Technology is not only inevitable and here to stay, it will continually evolve as new synchronous and asynchronous technologies emerge and as we use and shape them. How will we be able to grasp the features of all of these technologies—their benefits and limitations—and design for their most effective use? It is possible. Here are a dozen suggestions from our experience and our continual research and development.

1. Plan and design to develop methods that align your organization's and learners' needs with the dynamic learning environment;

2. Focus on the new technologies in an informal way, play with them, learn about their features and brainstorm their possibilities, and become aware of their limitations;

3. Distance yourself from the technologies by focusing on your organization, its needs and its objectives;

4. Look at your personnel and your budget;

5. Find the right blend and balance of synchronous and asynchronous technologies;

6. Develop policies and integrate them;

7. Develop awareness and acceptance with all of your stakeholders;

8. Train and support your staff, and be mindful of full accessibility;

9. Orient and support your learners; challenge and engage them;

10. Monitor continually to update and refine your program;

11. Create effective practices, lessons learned, and practical tips for sharing;

12. Realize and accept the fact that the only constant is change and that you are agents, not victims, of change.

GLOSSARY

Companion Web Site:
http://www.uwex.edu/disted/training/pubs/147tips/glossary.htm

ADA

The Americans with Disabilities Act, passed in 1990, requires businesses and educational institutions to be sensitive to special needs and to provide facility and program access.

Asynchronous

Video and data signals and devices that are not precisely in step, are not of the same frequency, or are not happening together in time.

Bio Sheet

A sheet or form designed by the instructor that is filled out by program or course participants and the instructor to provide professional and informal information for sharing.

Blended Technologies

The use of the appropriate technologies to meet specific objectives and needs. With a wide range available—from videoconferencing, web-conferencing, webcasting, instant messaging, podcasting, blogs, wikis, and gaming on the high-end to email, fax machines, and the telephone on the low-end—today's instructional leaders have a wealth of technologies to use for blending.

Blogs

Personal or group web spaces that provide for online commentary and links with areas for response from online readers. Blogs may be password protected or freely accessed, depending upon the author's preference. Vendors provide the web area and instructions for creating the blogs.

Chunking

Breaking instructional information into 10- to 15-minute chunks for the purpose of engaging students, holding their attention, and providing variety during a program or course.

Cognitive Component

The field of psychology has designated three components within the perceptual process: cognitive, affective, and psychomotor (behavioral). The cognitive component has long been emphasized in teaching and learning. Recent research is recognizing the importance and the inseparability of all three components.

Collaboration Tools

Software applications that are designed to help individuals within groups collaborate on common projects. In the technology environment, videoconferencing, webconferencing, and wikis fall into this category.

Constructivist Approach

This approach is based on the idea that learners are active agents in seeking meaning and, as such, construct their own knowledge. This knowledge becomes increasingly more complex, more finely differentiated, and more realistic, over time.

Contingency Plan

A plan that provides instructions for problem-solving in the event something happens by chance. A contingency plan is often called Plan B.

Copyright

This is a form of protection for authors of original works; a set of rights that regulate the use of particular ideas or the expression of information. It is one of the laws covered by intellectual property and gives owners the exclusive right to do and to authorize others to reproduce copies, prepare derivative works, and distribute, perform, and display these works publicly.

Copyright Audit List

This document lists all of the items within a book, production, or course that will need copyright clearance.

Creative Commons

The Creative Commons is a recently developed non-profit organization that is devoted to expanding the range of *creative* work legally available for others, to build upon and share. The organization releases copyright licenses known as *Creative Commons licenses*.

Distance Education

A planned teaching/learning experience that uses a wide spectrum of technologies to reach learners at a distance and is designed to encourage learner interaction and certification of learning. Also called distance teaching and learning.

Emotional Component

The field of psychology has designated three components within the perceptual process: cognitive, affective, and psychomotor (behavioral). The emotional component has long been neglected in teaching and learning. Recent research is recognizing its importance and the inseparability of all three components.

Evaluation

The systematic appraisal of the worth or value of something, someone, or a situation. Evaluation includes both formative (used during a program or course) and summative (used at the program or course conclusion).

508 Guidelines

A 1998 amendment to the Rehabilitation Act that requires federal agencies to make all electronic and information technology accessible to people with disabilities. This amendment was enacted to eliminate barriers, create new opportunities, and encourage the development of technologies that would assist people with disabilities.

Fair Use

This doctrine allows limited use, without permission from the rights holders, of copyrighted material. It is based on the rights of free speech and is unique to the United States.

Feedback

An integral part of the evaluation process, often called formative evaluation. By taking advantage of feedback opportunities, instructors can receive input from students that will refine the course. Instructors also provide feedback to students to help them realize change and modify learning.

Fiber Optics

These fibers, glass strands as fine as a human hair, are rapidly replacing copper wire and are revolutionizing electronic communications: video, audio, and the Internet. They provide digital data transmission at a high rate over a distance.

Guest Experts

Often instructors have the need for additional expertise within their program or course. It is common for them to ask guest experts to participate and provide their special expertise. Guest experts should always be provided with an orientation to the technology they will be using.

Help Desk

The information and assistance center for helping to trouble shoot problems that occur during distance education programs and courses. The Help Desk is reached either by a toll-free number, a web site, or email. Help Desks may also offer other user services and are also used outside of distance education.

HTML

This acronym stands for HyperText Markup Language. HTML is the formatting used for the World Wide Web.

Instant Messaging (IM)

Real-time messaging, using typed electronic text between two or more people. The messages are conveyed via computers connected over the Internet or other networks.

Instructional Design

Effective teaching via distance education doesn't just happen, it happens—by design. Instructional design is both an art and a science. An effective instructional design process focuses on the learner and course objectives, the appropriate selection and use of technology or blended technologies, support, formats and strategies, interaction activities, and integrated evaluation. It engages the learner and takes the entire course experience into consideration to help meet goals that are both practical and effective.

Instructional Designer

The instructional designer applies instructional design theory and experience to the design process and guides faculty and staff in the overall development of the course or program. This process includes a focus on the learner, a content overview, the selection of appropriate technologies, the development of a timeline and support team, the scope and sequence of the content, the development of interaction opportunities, the development of materials, and the integration of feedback and evaluation.

Instructor Console

In videoconferencing and webcasting, instructors usually teach from an instructor console. The console is a desk or podium that contains all of the electronic equipment and connections that the instructor needs to facilitate the session or sessions. Consoles should be constructed to be disability accessible.

Interactive Approach

An interactive approach is designed to engage learners in their learning process. It incorporates activities, projects, and processes that provide learners with a true sense of participation. The interactive approach is instrumental in retaining student attention.

ISDN

Integrated Services Digital Network (ISDN) is a digital copper wire telephone system that transmits voice and data, resulting in high quality and high speeds over regular phone lines. In videoconferencing, ISDN is used to provide voice, video, and text between individual and group videoconferencing systems.

Internet

A decentralized global network of computers that lets people dialog and exchange news and data. The Internet can be accessed in a wide variety of ways through Internet services. The Internet is not the "same" as the World Wide Web.

iPod®

An electronic pod created by Apple® that enables podcasting (a web feed of audio or video files placed on the Internet) for anyone with an iPod® to subscribe to. The subscription feeds will automatically deliver new content to the iPod® when connected to a computer.

Kolb Learning Style Inventory

This instrument describes the way people learn and the way they deal with daily situations. It is based on the work of John Dewey, Kurt Lewin, Jean Piaget, and others.

Learner-Centered Approach

Learner-centered education places the learner at the center of the educational experience and places the learning responsibility on the learner. In this approach, learner educational contexts are taken into consideration and instructors facilitate the learning and evaluate the student's progress towards learning objectives. By learners acquiring skills to learn, it provides a basis for life-long learning.

LMS

Learning Management System (LMS), also called Course Management System (CMS), provides a course shell and features for developing and containing online programs and courses.

Mnemonic Devices

Memory aides or devices that assist in remembering meaningful information. Mnemonics can take the form of a short poem, song, word list, or association.

Mobile Devices

Handheld computers that are small enough to hold in your hand. They are also called personal digital assistants (PDAs). Input is via small keyboards, handwriting, or touch screens. They are used for storing information (data and video) and accessing the Internet and WWW.

MP3 Player

MP3 is the name of a type of file. The player is a portable device that stores digital music and organizes and plays these files. An MP3 player can often use other files (e.g., Windows Media Audio).

Multiple Intelligences

Identified by Howard Gardner of Harvard University, multiple intelligences suggest that intelligence is more than IQ. Gardner initially proposed seven different intelligences in children and adults. He has expanded the number to nine: linguistic, logical, spatial, kinesthetic, musical, interpersonal, intrapersonal, naturalistic, and spiritual.

Murphy's Law

According to Murphy's Law, anything that can go wrong will go wrong; errors will inevitably occur. As it applies to distance education, an environment with numerous variables, it is essential to understand and plan for as many variables as possible and also have a contingency plan, a Plan B.

Myers–Briggs Type Indicator

This indicator identifies personal preferences. It was developed during World War II and follows criteria from the work of Carl Jung.

Online Tutorials

Documents posted online that have been created to provide instruction for individuals or groups who need training or specific information. These documents often include graphics and animation, in addition to text.

Origination Site

The location and facility from which the instructor or instructors teach via technology.

Pager

An electronic device that alerts the carrier with a series of beeps or vibrations, notifying the person that there is a message.

PDF

Portable Document Format (PDF) is a computer file format used to publish and distribute electronic documents that include text, image, animation, or multimedia. The layout, formatting, and all attributes remain as the original. Special software is required to view the documents.

Perceptual Learning

This approach is based on the idea of humans as perceivers within their environments. Perceptual learning includes an emphasis on sense awareness within environments, attention, and differentiation, resulting in heightened awareness. Perceptual learning is a process of discovery and enrichment over time.

Polls

A method for providing feedback by voting on a series of questions. Polls are often integrated into software and are used extensively in web-conferencing, webcasting, and online.

Portfolios

In distance education, students are increasingly being asked to collect, organize, and manage their program or course work (text, files, images, webwork, and projects) in a portfolio format. These portfolios are often referred to as e-Portfolios or electronic portfolios.

Post-Test

Testing after an educational program or course for comparison with the pre-test to determine what a student has learned or gained in experience and knowledge.

PowerPoint®

Presentation software that has become very popular for preparing slides that can be projected in "in-room" presentations and via technology. This software includes numerous presentation features: audio, animation, handout, notes, and print capability.

Pre-Test

Advance testing. A test given prior to a learning experience that is designed to determine a student's knowledge and experience for an educational program or course.

Presentation Skills

A presenter is really an instrument of expression. All instruments need to be fine-tuned. Presenters must pay close attention to their learners, listen, and use voice, facial expressions, and gestures to enhance their presentation or teaching situation. In addition, they need to personalize and engage their learners by providing opportunities for participation. Presentation skills are especially important in the virtual environment, where instructors and learners are separated.

Profile

A format for students and instructors to fill in for sharing professional and personal information. Profiles are often used by students and instructors in the distance learning environment. Profiles are an integral part of some LMS software.

Protocol

Ground rules developed by the instructor to ensure that the program or course runs smoothly. These rules include etiquette—thinking of others and treating everyone with respect.

Psychomotor Component

The field of psychology has designated three components within the perceptual process: cognitive, affective, and psychomotor (behavioral). The cognitive component has long been emphasized in teaching and learning. Recent research is recognizing the importance and the inseparability of all three components.

Questionnaires

A format that contains a series of questions that will provide either qualitative or quantitative information to the person or organization collecting the information.

Remote Sites

Locations at which students meet for learning and interaction via technology. Sites may be either group or individual locations.

Role-Play

To take the part of a real or fictional person and act out in a scenario.

Satellite Videoconferencing

One-way video and audio delivered via satellite to multiple remote sites; telephone, fax, and/or a key pad supply the means for interaction.

Scientific Calculator

A device used by students, engineers, and accountants for performing basic mathematical calculations and plotting simple graphics.

Scope and Sequence

A curriculum framework that looks at the overall scope of a program or course and the sequence of the content from beginning to end.

Simulations

A simulation creates the appearance of being real, giving the experience of a real situation without the risks.

Site Coordinators

The person designated to be in charge at remote distance education sites. They are the eyes, ears, hands, and feet of the origination site instructor and are critical to the success of distance education experiences.

Special Needs

This term describes people who need special assistance in any situation. In distance education it may mean providing special software or hardware, room accommodations, room personnel, or course materials.

Support Personnel

All those who support the distance education experience: administrative, instructional design, graphic design, web design, technical, library, and site personnel.

Surveys

A method for gathering information from a general population for the purpose of gaining qualitative or quantitative information on a designated topic.

Syllabus

A document that summarizes all of the component parts of a program or course that includes an introduction, all instructions, assignments, and grading process, as well as contact information.

Synchronous Technologies

Video and data signals and devices that are precisely in step, are of the same frequency, and are happening together in time.

Traditional Classroom

Traditional face-to-face teaching and learning with the instructor and learners in the same room.

Timeline

Lists all details of pre-planning, planning, developing, implementing, and evaluating to ensure that every component of the program is given adequate time for preparation and implementation.

Trademark

A unique term, symbol, or image used by an individual or organization to identify its products and differentiate them from those of other individuals or organizations. A trademark is a type of intellectual property and usually includes a name, term, symbol, design, image, or a combination of these.

URL

This acronym stands for Uniform Resource Locator. It is the World Wide Web (WWW) address for finding documents and resources on the WWW. The first part of the address (e.g., ftp://www or http://www) describes the Internet protocol to be used and the second part (e.g., uwex.edu) indicates the Internet address or domain name.

Videoconferencing

Videoconferencing is two-way interactive and falls into several categories: (1) full motion video and audio delivered via microwave or a fiber optic network; (2) compressed video in which the bandwidth of the images and sound are compressed through a coding/decoding process, delivered over special dial-up phone lines and decompressed at the receive sites; and (3) compressed Internet Protocol (IP) video and audio, delivered over the Internet. All types of videoconferencing can interface with a wide variety of technologies and media.

Virtual Classroom

The virtual space into which participants at a distance are brought together and in which participants are actually present visually and audibly.

Virtual Presence

A sense of "being there" is critical to the success of designing, teaching, and learning at a distance using both synchronous and asynchronous technologies. Until recently, presence has been defined and discussed in terms of behavioral or cognitive theory. Emotional aspects of presence have been largely ignored. Obtaining virtual presence is the result of incorporating emotions and taking into consideration their interaction with behavior and cognition.

Webcasting

Webcasting is a fully integrated system that allows for the capture and recording of audio, video, and data, such as PowerPoint® slides, in one streamed media presentation. It automatically syncs a speaker's video with the delivery of his or her support data—such as graphics, slides, videotapes, or DVDs—into one single, seamless presentation. Webcasting can be presented live or archived for future use.

Webconferencing

Webconferencing is a synchronous, interactive communication between two or more computers via the Web. It may include the transmission of text, graphics, files, voice, and motion video. Voice transmission may be achieved through a telephone bridge or via the webconferencing product. As connection speeds increase and standards improve, more companies are integrating voice and video capabilities into their products. Many also provide the capability to record meetings and play them back at a later time.

Wiki

Wiki is pronounced "wee-kee" and is named after the Hawaiian term "wiki wiki" meaning "quick." Wikis are group-centered, project oriented web spaces and are usually password protected. They make publishing, sharing, and editing content very easy. Vendors provide the web location and instructions for creation of wikis.

WWW

The World Wide Web (WWW) is a network of networks, consisting of Internet servers that support specially formatted HTML (HyperText Markup Language) documents. Links within the documents connect to other documents, graphics, audio, and video files.

REFERENCES

Companion Web Site:
http://www.uwex.edu/disted/training/pubs/147tips/re_citations.htm

ADA Information Center. 2007. Provides training, information, and technical assistance on the Americans with Disabilities Act (ADA) to businesses, consumers, and the state and local governments. Retrieved January 19, 2007, from www.adainfo.org.

Americans with Disabilities Act Document Center. 2007. *ADA statute, regulations, ADAAG* (Americans with Disabilities Act Accessibility Guidelines). Tech sheets, documents, and links to sources of information: Retrieved January 19, 2007, from www.jan.wvu.edu/links/ adalinks.htm.

Copyright Clearance Center. 2007. Retrieved January 19, 2007, from www.copy right.com.

Creative Commons web site. 2007. Retrieved January 19, 2007, from http:// creativecommons. org/.

Department of Justice ADA Home Page. 2007. The ADA Home Page provides access to Americans with Disabilities Act (ADA) regulations for businesses and State and local governments, technical assistance materials. *ADA standards*. Retrieved January 15, 2007, from www.usdoj. gov/crt/ada/adahom1.htm.

Electronic and Information Technology (Section 508) Homepage. 2007. Retrieved January 15, 2007, from www.access-board.gov/508.htm.

ERVING Network Student Contract. 2007. Retrieved March 20, 2007, from www.erving. k12.wi.us/student%20contract.doc.

Gardner, H. 1993. *Multiple intelligences: The theory in practice*. Basic Books: New York.

Gibson, C. 1998. *Distance learners in higher education: Institutional responses for quality outcomes*. Madison, WI: Atwood Publishing.

Harris, P., Moran, R. and Moran, S. 2004. *Managing cultural differences*. Sixth Edition. Linacre House, Oxford, UK: Jordan Hill.

Kolb Learning Style Inventory. 2007. Retrieved January 5, 2007, from www.algon quin college.com /edtech/gened/styles.html.

Lehman, R. 2000. *Characteristics of a successful distance education instructor*. Handout developed for Instructional Communications Systems, University of Wisconsin-Extension, Madison.

Lehman, R. 2001. *The essential videoconferencing guide: 7 keys to success*. Madison, WI: Instructional Communications Systems, University of Wisconsin-Extension.

Lehman, R. 2003. *The dynamic learner*. Www.uwex.edu/disted/training/sevenkeys/companion/dynamic.htm.

Lehman, R. 2006. The role of emotion in creating instructor and learner presence in the distance education experience. *Journal of Cognitive Affective Learning* 2(2).

Lehman, R., Dewey, B., and Berg, R. 2002. *Using distance education technologies: Effective practices*. Madison: Instructional Communications Systems, University of Wisconsin-Extension.

Moore, M. 1989. Three types of interaction. *The American Journal of Distance Education* 3(2).

Mutliple Intelligences Survey. 2007. Retrieved January 5, 2007, from http://surfaquarium.com/ MI/inventory.htm.

Myers–Briggs Type Indicator. 2007. Retrieved January 4, 2007, from www.knowyourtype. com/mbti.html.

Noe, A. 2005. *Action in perception*. Cambridge, MA: MIT Press.

U.S. Rehabilitation Act. 2007. Official web site for Section 508. Retrieved January 19, 2007, from www.section508.gov.

WebAIM Section 508 Checklist. 2007. Retrieved January 19, 2007, from www.webaim.org/standards/508/checklist.php.

THE AUTHORS

Rosemary M. Lehman is Senior Outreach/Distance Education Specialist and Manager of the Instructional Design Team at Instructional Communications Systems (ICS), University of Wisconsin-Extension (UWEX). She has over 30 years experience in media production, design elements, and professional development and has been with UWEX for 16 years. Rosemary holds a Ph.D. in Distance Education/Adult Learning, an M.A. in Television/Communication Arts from University of Wisconsin–Madison, and a B.A. in English from Lawrence College (University), Appleton, WI. In her work at ICS she conducts sessions on program design, development, and implementation using blended technologies; creates and publishes professional development materials, journal articles, and book chapters. Rosemary has also authored and edited several books. She coordinates distance education seminars and conferences, as well as keynotes and presents at a wide variety of conferences statewide, nationally, and internationally. She is the recipient of a Consortium of College and University Media Centers (CCUMC) Research Award and the UW-Extension Award for Excellence in education, technology, and leadership.

Richard A. Berg is Instructional Design and Distance Education Specialist with ICS and has over eight years experience in training materials production, instructional development, media production, and training. He holds a M.S. in Instructional Technology and Telecommunications and a B.A. in English Education from Western Illinois University in Macomb. Rich also trains University of Wisconsin faculty and State of Wisconsin Governmental Agency employees in the use of videoconferencing and webconferencing technologies. He designed and maintains the web sites for Instructional Design, Training for Videoconferencing, DESIEN Archives, and the companion web sites for *Using Distance Education Technology: Effective Practices* (Lehman, Dewey, and Berg 2002), *The Essential Videoconferencing Guide: 7 Keys to Success* (Lehman 2001), and the companion web site for this book. Rich has been published in *College and University Media Review*, presented at the Annual Conference on Distance Teaching and Learning in Madison, Wisconsin, and been accepted to present at the 2007 annual conference of the Association for Educational Communications and Technology (AECT).

NOTES

NOTES

NOTES